COLLABORATIVE PROGRAM PLANNING

Principles, Practices, and Strategies

The Professional Practices in Adult Education and Human Resource Development Series explores issues and concerns of practitioners who work in the broad range of settings in adult and continuing education and human resource development.

The books are intended to provide information and strategies on how to make practice more effective for professionals and those they serve. They are written from a practical viewpoint and provide a forum for instructors, administrators, policy makers, counselors, trainers, managers, program and organizational developers, instructional designers, and other related professionals.

Editorial correspondence should be sent to the Editor-in-Chief:

Michael W. Galbraith
Florida Atlantic University
Department of Educational Leadership
College of Education
Boca Raton, FL 33431

COLLABORATIVE PROGRAM PLANNING

Principles, Practices, and Strategies

Joe F. Donaldson

Charles E. Kozoll

KRIEGER PUBLISHING COMPANY
MALABAR, FLORIDA
1999

Original Edition 1999

Printed and Published by
KRIEGER PUBLISHING COMPANY
KRIEGER DRIVE
MALABAR, FLORIDA 32950

Library of Congress Cataloging-In-Publication Data

Donaldson, Joe F.
Collaborative program planning : principles, practices, and strategies / Joe F. Donaldson, Charles E. Kozoll. — Original ed.
p. cm. — (Professional practices in adult education and human resource development series)
Includes bibliographical references (p.) and index.
ISBN 1-57524-012-2 (alk. paper)
1. Adult education—Planning. 2. Continuing education—Planning. 3. Occupational training—Planning. 4. Education, Cooperative—Planning. I. Kozoll, Charles E. II. Title. III. Series.
LC5225.E57D66 1999
374.12—dc21 98-30740
CIP

10 9 8 7 6 5 4 3 2

CONTENTS

PREFACE

Collaboration in various forms has become an increasingly evident and important way for work of all kinds to be conducted. Each day we read about new joint ventures of two or more manufacturing companies that join forces to develop a new product or efforts of several governmental units to cooperate to reduce expenses. In the auto industry competitors may work together to produce a new car model that combines the excellent features of its diverse producers. Large industries have ongoing relationships with smaller businesses that supply products and services needed "just-in-time." Increasingly among local governments, agreements are being made to share services that are too costly for single jurisdictions. Two small communities may purchase a fire engine jointly, share emergency services, or agree to help each other with road maintenance.

A lesson to be learned from these examples is that "going alone" is less and less common, and logical. To survive and succeed, organizations of all kinds, in public and private sectors, are collaborating. Working together can be a very brief arrangement, for one small event, or a major joint venture involving millions of dollars and protracted negotiations.

In this book, we focus on a particular kind of collaboration that is becoming increasingly common: not-for-profit organizations working together to plan and offer educational programs for adults. Our initial investigations revealed seven reasons for this trend, reasons that will be examined in more detail throughout this book.

Competition for participants is much greater, as more organizations offer educational programs. Today, for example, we are witnessing a substantial growth in the number of continuing professional education programs for individuals in all fields, because of the rapid expansion of information, changes in laws, and alterations in practice. Because of this expansion in available programs, sponsors that previously offered programs alone are combining efforts. A hospital, an allied health group, and a community college are one such combination, working together on programs for medical technologists or respiratory therapists. There are other such combinations in continuing professional education where a graduate educational institution and one or more professional societies regularly offer joint programs.

Staying closer to practitioners is a second reason for increased cooperation. Professionals will be more likely to attend a program when they know that it is planned by those who understand practice. A program for maintenance engineers that has been successful for nearly 50 years is planned by representatives of those who will attend and by those in government agencies whose information is of great value to the participants. A program for civil engineers has a similar longevity for the very same reason. By including practitioners, both programs have established a great deal of credibility.

Financial risk is the third reason collaboration has become so much more attractive today. Individual sponsors often strain to invest the capital that new programs, in particular, require. Spreading financial risk among several sponsors reduces the burden each must carry and makes the possibility of failure somewhat less imposing. Recently, a university continuing education department and a professional association worked together to offer a seminar series on developing local educational foundations. Although interest in the program had been expressed, the level of attendance was uncertain. There were fixed expenses that had to be paid, for example, for production of a brochure and postage. However, neither sponsor had to provide money up front, since a conference unit handled the administrative arrangements. Both cosponsors had agreed to cover any deficit; actually, each realized a small profit.

Prestige through association is another advantage of collaboration. Having the name of one or more well-known and respected organizations on promotional material lends credibility to programs. Obviously, this form of support indicates trust on the part of cosponsors in what will be presented at the program. In some cases, partner organizations will provide access to speakers or to other resources that are not generally accessible to a single partner. The world affairs programs offered annually in a number of small Midwestern cities are cosponsored by major companies located in the communities, educational institutions, and local foundations. This has proven to be a strong and long-term partnership, that has offered successful programs for nearly 25 years. Equally impressive is this partnership's track record in attracting as program speakers prominent national and international experts. The ability to attract this caliber of speaker to small communities is very much a function of both the prestige of the different collaborating organizations and the programs' reputation for success.

Programs with many committed cosponsors have "champions," who will work hard to see that the program succeeds. They will market the program to their members and strongly encourage attendance. Representatives of individual sponsors may accept responsibility for certain portions of the program. The facilities of one sponsor may be made available at no cost; another sponsor may cover costs of copying materials, and a third may provide staff assistance to handle participant registration. Mailing lists of partner organizations are routinely made available. When planners meet, other ways to make the program a success can be identified. The whole becomes far greater than the sum of its parts.

Groups working together are more attractive to those who may provide funds to support a program. A foundation, individual donor, or public agency may be more comfortable supporting a joint effort. The success potential has been increased because more individuals from different organizations are enthusiastic about the program and willing to work hard on it. That includes finding funds to support the program. With a diverse group of champions, the ability to locate needed dollars increases.

Finally, cosponsored programs can withstand difficult times with greater resilience than those offered by a single sponsor. There are a number of reasons for this ability. There is increased access to funds to support a program experiencing some decline in attendance. In addition, a collaborative group, in contrast to a single provider, has the potential for generating more ideas about how a program can be made more attractive or how costs can be reduced. Most of all, there is the collective will to sustain a program by reconfiguring it in some way to make it more competitive and relevant.

However, for the advantages of collaboration to be realized, those participating must have a good understanding of how successful relationships are developed. This requires attention to a variety of subtle processes and tensions involved in such an undertaking. It is to the understanding of these processes and tensions, and strategies for dealing with them, that this book is dedicated.

By including insights drawn from interviews with adult and continuing educators, this book relies not only on theory. Rather, it also taps the implicit, practical know-how of practitioners who grapple with issues of collaboration on a day-to-day basis. As a result, the book joins theory with practical knowledge, the form of knowledge that has increasingly been recognized as being central to effective program planning practice.

In addition, most sociological, organizational, business, and even adult and continuing education literature has focused, to date, almost exclusively on decisions about when to collaborate. Much less attention has been paid to the development and maintenance of collaborative relationships once the initial decision to engage in them has been made. This book is different from this earlier literature in that while it draws upon the earlier material in the literature, it also gives much greater notice to the factors surrounding the development and maintenance of collaborative arrangements, as well as to elements to be considered when relationships begin to deteriorate, become fragile, and perhaps should be terminated.

OVERVIEW OF CONTENTS

In the opening chapter the theoretical foundations for collaborative program planning are described by reviewing the literature on interorganizational collaboration and linking insights from this literature to the planning and provision of educational programs for adults. Five major ideas about collaboration are introduced and discussed in this chapter, as are several frameworks that contribute to understanding and making decisions about collaboration. The chapters which follow build on this theoretical foundation by examining examples of collaboration by practitioners in seven not-for-profit, adult and continuing education settings. Chapter 2 presents a transition between theory and practice by providing a backdrop and grounding for the richness of practitioner insights and experiences which are related in remaining chapters. The settings in which the practitioners work are described. The processes we used to select practitioners to interview, to gather information from them, and to analyze the information they shared are also detailed in Chapter 2.

The roles of *leadership* and *vision* are examined in Chapter 3. These two topics are closely related. Leaders are essential for any program planning effort to commence and continue. Different leadership roles will be required at different times from different people involved in the collaborative effort. Leadership roles identified in the literature and from our interviews with practitioners are described in this chapter. One function of leadership is to work with others to develop a vision that guides the collaborative relationship as the program is planned. Vision plays other roles in collaboration and these are also addressed in this chapter.

The *tensions* and *transformations* of collaboration are the focus of Chapter 4. Examples from practitioners' experiences are used to demonstrate how competing forces create a range of tensions that must be balanced if collaboration is to be effective. The types of transformations that may be experienced during collaboration are also covered in this chapter. In addition, we take special note of changes that affect collaborative relationships negatively and identify several signs that point to increased stress in and potential fragility of these relationships.

While Chapter 4 raises awareness and sensitivity to the tensions and transformations of collaborative relationships,

Chapter 5 describes *strategies for dealing with these tensions and transformations.* Strategies addressed include monitoring the relationship, building trust and communicating, and dealing with differences. In Chapter 5 we also address strategies that may be used to dissolve relationships if they become fragile and cannot, or should not, be sustained.

In Chapter 6 attention is turned to the *assessment* of collaborative programming prior to, during, and after a program has been developed and offered. The intensity of collaboration required in planning varies with the complexity of programming to be accomplished and other situational factors, including elements of specific practice settings. The aspects of programming that characterize different levels of program complexity are identified and described in this chapter. Also considered is the assessment of program complexity and the use of its results to guide judgments about the intensity of collaboration required. Other factors that need evaluation in collaborative programming are also identified in this chapter.

In Chapter 7 attention is focused on the *interconnected dynamics of program development and collaboration.* This chapter provides an opportunity to revisit major themes that have been addressed earlier in the book. But, the chapter goes beyond mere recapitulation to present several major conclusions about the connection between the processes of collaboration and program development.

AUDIENCE

This book is intended primarily for adult and continuing educators who develop programs for adults in a variety of not-for-profit settings, but it also has broader application. We have drawn our examples from several program planning contexts in which adult and continuing educators work. These settings include a park district, a distance education consortium, a local government training program, a private consulting firm, a major professional association, a staff development organization, and a university graduate department. The book will have particular relevance to those who practice in these and similar settings. But we also believe that, since issues related to collaboration cut across practice settings, the ideas addressed will be of much value to those who work in different arenas. Because the book attends to both theory and practice, highlighting the interconnection between the two in the provision of educational programs for adults, it is also intended for those who teach, study, and do research on program planning and/or collaboration among not-for-profit organizations.

In many ways, collaboration is similar to the simultaneous spinning of plates common among circus performers. Every plate has to be started and then kept in motion. To keep the plates in motion, the circus performer has to run back in forth, giving each needed attention. None of the plates can be forgotten; not only could one fall, but all could collapse because of a lack of attention to one. Such is the reality of collaborative program development and delivery. Although several major themes will be explored in remaining chapters, each theme is related to all others. The themes themselves and the subthemes that they encompass must all be addressed together for a collaborative effort to grow and be sustained.

Joe F. Donaldson,
Columbia, Missouri

Charles E. Kozoll,
Champaign, Illinois

ACKNOWLEDGMENTS

We appreciate the contributions of a number of people who helped us a great deal as this book was conceived, written, and shaped. The book would not have been possible without the assistance of eight practitioners who shared their experiences with us about collaborative program planning. Their insights, observations, and willingness to stay in contact with us throughout the process and to openly and honestly describe their good and bad experiences with collaboration were essential. They not only contributed significantly to the book but also to our own understanding of the collaborative process. Although they remain anonymous, our sincere and deep appreciation goes to them for their invaluable assistance with this project. Michael Galbraith provided us clear guidance throughout the project and served as an excellent sounding board as the book was conceived and completed. The Krieger staff, especially Marie Bowles, were particularly helpful as the book was being prepared for production.

We are also indebted to a number of valued colleagues who reviewed the book. These included Jim Lyon, Virginia Miller, Meredith Donaldson, Sean Flynt, Elaine Mondschein, Barbara Brandt, and Philip Swain. As a result of their perceptive comments and useful suggestions, the book has been strengthened in innumerable ways.

Thanks go to our families, and especially to our wives and children whose support, patience, encouragement, and wise counsel contributed much to the book and its completion. Finally to all those who collaborate goes our thanks for inspiring us to attack this important and demanding strategy for planning and offering educational programs for adults.

THE AUTHORS

Joe F. Donaldson is an associate professor in the Department of Educational Leadership and Policy Analysis at the University of Missouri-Columbia. In this role, Donaldson teaches courses on the adult learner, organization and administration of higher and continuing education, program planning, and continuing education for the professions. His current research and writing focus on continuing education for the professions, particularly the impact of organizational and practice contexts on professional learning and performance, and the organization, administration, and leadership of continuing higher education. He has addressed these topics in over seventy publications, including refereed journal articles, books, book chapters, and research and technical reports. Donaldson has made over 80 peer-reviewed and invited-paper presentations in these areas at technical and professional meetings.

From 1987 to 1991 Donaldson served on the adult education faculty at The Pennsylvania State University. Prior to that, he was head of the Division of Extramural courses at the University of Illinois at Urbana-Champaign, and worked in the Office of University Outreach in the University of Wisconsin System.

He has chaired the University Continuing Education Association's (UCEA) Council for Continuing Education Management and Administration and served on UCEA's Board of Directors. He also has served as chair of the Serial Publications Committee of the American Association for Adult and Continuing Education, assistant editor of the *American Journal of Distance Education*, editorial board member for the *Continuing Higher Education Review*, and chair of UCEA's Advisory Committee for its publication series on organizational issues in continuing higher education. Currently, Donaldson serves on the Editorial Boards of the *Journal of Continuing Higher Education*, and the *International Journal of Continuing Education Practice*, and as secretary-treasurer of UCEA's Division of Research.

Donaldson has received numerous awards for research and publications from the UCEA, and has been a recipient of awards for outstanding teaching at several institutions. Several grants and contracts have supported his research on continuing professional education and the organization and administration of continuing higher education.

Donaldson has served as consultant to several organizations, including the Institute of Food Technologists, the National Health Service Corps, the Judicial Education Committee of the State of Missouri, the Michigan Coordinating Council on Continuing Higher Education, the Society of Real Estate Appraisers, and The Pennsylvania State University. In this role, he has worked with organizations in the areas of organizational change, continuing professional education, and strategic planning.

Donaldson is the author of *Managing Credit Programs in Continuing Higher Education* and UCEA's publication, *Continuing Education Reviews: Principles, Practices and Strategies.* He holds a B.S. and M.S. from the University of Tennessee-Knoxville and a Ph.D. in continuing education from the University of Wisconsin-Madison.

Charles E. Kozoll is a professor of education and associate director of the Office of Continuing Education and Public Service (OCEPS) at the University of Illinois at Urbana-Champaign. In these positions, he has major administrative responsibility for a number of continuing education programs, in addition to teaching and advising masters and doctoral students. Kozoll's course areas are program planning and evaluation and human resource development. He has taught the course on program development in continuing education for the past 20 years.

In his role as associate director of OCEPS, he serves as editor of two publication series and assists in the development of noncredit programs for professional audiences. He also initiated Elderhostel programs at the university and a number of other programs for seniors. His most recent work involves study of how results of research can be provided to lay audiences in an understandable and useful form.

With a background in both adult learning and organizational psychology, Kozoll has worked closely with a number of private and public organizations to evaluate employee productivity, to present supervisory training programs, and to prepare a variety of training materials. His clients have included local, state, and federal government agencies, social service organizations, small product and service businesses, and educational institutions. He serves as a national lecturer on productivity for Phi Delta Kappa and is an associate in the Executive Development Center at the University of Illinois at Urbana-Champaign.

In addition to consulting, Kozoll has written on a variety of management-related topics with emphasis on training a new employees, time and stress management, and developing supervisory skills. He has published eight books, over 200 articles, six software programs, and a videotape on time and stress management. His material has appeared in the publications of Dartnell Corporation, Bureau of Business Practice, the National Management Institute and The Alexander Hamilton Institute. He is the coauthor of recent publications on: Activity-Based Costing, Decision-Making in Higher Education, and Program Development in Continuing Education.

His degrees from the University of Michigan, Boston University, and Columbia University are in the areas of political science, adult learning, and organizational psychology.

CHAPTER 1

The Theoretical Foundations of Collaboration

The purpose of this book is to join theory and practice as an overall guide to those in a variety of not-for-profit organizations who must collaborate in both ordinary and difficult circumstances in the development and delivery of educational programs for adults. Collaboration is increasingly being employed by all types of organizations to achieve a variety of objectives. As a consequence of the growth of such efforts, there has been an attendant increase in the volume of literature that addresses the reasons for and dynamics of collaboration. However, this book differs from earlier literature and the growing volume of current literature in three important ways. First, this book addresses the use of collaboration as a strategy in the development and delivery of educational programs for adults by those working in the not-for-profit sector. Most current literature deals with the subject from the perspective of the profit sector with little coverage of providing educational programs for adults.

Second, this book places equal or greater weight on the processes associated with the development and maintenance of collaborative relationships. Most previous literature, even the adult and continuing education literature, has focused almost entirely on factors associated with decisions to collaborate in the first place. What has been missing is discussion of the dynamics and actions involved in building and sustaining relationships once the decision has been made, or of factors to be considered when relationships begin to deteriorate and become fragile ones. By concentrating on these latter areas, this book addresses some critical elements that, while not a focus of the majority of literature, nonetheless have an equal or greater impact on the success and quality of educational programs, the eventual products of collaboration.

Third, this book intends to join theory with practice. Although the literature certainly provides insights about adult and continuing education practice, it is still highly theoretical and abstract. This book brings theory to life through examples from the experiences of several practitioners to demonstrate how concepts and dynamics manifest themselves in different practice settings. By drawing on practitioner experience, theory is not only brought to life, but is elaborated and deepened by the insights gained from practitioners about the strategies they employ to collaborate successfully in real practice settings.

In order to benefit fully from the insights of practitioners, we must first have an understanding of the theoretical foundations of collaborative practice. In this chapter we summarize the literature on interorganizational collaboration and connect insights from the literature to the planning and provision of educational programs for adults. Key ideas about these types of arrangements will be identified, as will several frameworks that aid us in understanding and making decisions about them.

Several literature sources were employed in developing this review. The adult and continuing education literature comprised a portion of our review, but we did not rely solely upon it. Rather, we also drew extensively from the organizational, sociological, and business literature to identify concepts and factors that are important in decisions to enter a collaborative arrangement or partnership and to examine concepts and factors associated with the development, maintenance, and termination of these kinds of relationships.

KEY IDEAS

Five major ideas about collaboration come into major relief from a review of the literature:

- There are many different types of partnerships; however, these can be classified on a continuum based upon their level of intensity and degree of formality.
- Collaborative relationships among organizations are organizations themselves. However, they differ from conventional organizations because they have shorter life spans, employ unconventional kinds of governance, and rely more on informal mechanisms.
- Leadership is a critical variable in collaboration, and leadership roles and behaviors in these arrangements differ somewhat from those we usually associate with our own organizations.
- The creation and maintenance of collaborative relationships follow a developmental process that is characterized by distinct, although not necessarily discrete, developmental stages and by constant flux and transformation.
- Tensions between the formal and informal exist in every collaborative relationship. Maintenance and growth of the relationship depend upon preserving a delicate balance between the formality and informality of the relationship as negotiations proceed, commitments are made, as programs are implemented, and as the process and results are assessed.

Each of these key ideas is addressed in the sections that follow.

A CONTINUUM OF RELATIONSHIPS

The kinds of partnerships we will be describing in this book have been called different things in the literature—for example, collaborative arrangements, cooperative arrangements, interorganizational relationships, cosponsorship, and partnerships. We will be using these terms interchangeably in describing the variety of relationships detailed in this book, except in specific instances in which we will provide examples to illustrate a particular type.

Different types of collaborative relationships are also described in the literature. Kanter (1994) distinguished among three major types of relationships based upon the major purposes they serve: (a) mutual service consortia, in which organizations come together, for instance, to purchase equipment; (b) value-chain partnerships, in which suppliers and customers develop a relationship to achieve the complementary goals of ensuring markets for products and an uninterrupted supply of resources; and, (c) joint ventures, in which organizations enter partnerships to develop joint products or programs or to share markets for them. Although it is possible for educational organizations to enter into any one of these three types of partnerships, the focus of this book is on joint ventures for programming.

Partnerships can also be categorized on the basis of whether they are mandated or voluntary, and if voluntary, whether they are formal or informal. Mandated relationships are those that are required by law or regulation or stipulated as a condition of funding, as might be the case in a grant or contract for an educational program. Mandated partnerships tend to be formalized and guided by a legal contract, although they do not necessarily have to be. Voluntary relationships may be either formal or informal. Formal relationships may be characterized by legal contract, but they differ from mandated ones by their voluntary nature. Informal relationships are based primarily upon personal relationships among individuals representing the participating organizations. As will be seen in later sections of this chapter, a relationship can also be characterized by different levels of formality and informality. For example, in a formal partnership, the informal relationships among individual partners can still play a central role in the partnership's development.

Conversely, as informal relationships evolve over time, more formality may be needed, and this increased formality (perhaps in the form of a contract) will also be an important factor in the partnership's development. For example, four faculty members from four community colleges in a Midwestern state entered into an informal agreement to permit the transfer of course credits among their colleges. The community colleges were located close to each other, and this arrangement allowed students to enrich their programs of study by taking courses at the different community colleges. After a while, however, the leadership of the community colleges began to worry about what would happen to this informal, friendship-based agreement if one of the faculty members were to move. As a consequence, a course articulation contract among the four community colleges was developed, formalizing the arrangement. Although the evidence does not suggest that this formalization changed the nature of the relationship among the faculty, it did ensure the collaborative arrangement's long-term survival. What had begun as an informal agreement among friends had become institutionalized, establishing new parameters within which the partnership would continue. Therefore the mandated/voluntary and formal/informal characteristics of partnerships are important because they establish the parameters within which partnerships develop.

A central factor in considerations of interorganizational relationships is the degree to which organizations are interdependent. By "interdependence" we mean the degree to which (a) organizations take each other into account in pursuing their goals and (b) the organizations' growth and survival within the external environment are linked (Gray, 1989; Schermerhorn, 1975). Cervero (1988, 1992) used this concept to develop a typology of six orientations or strategies toward interdependence that may be employed by providers of educational programs for adults. The orientations are as follows:

1. Monopoly—In this case the adult education provider is the only one of its kind and has no competition from other providers. For example, as the only YWCA in the community, this not-for-profit agency provides the only programming directly related to leadership development for women.

2. Parallelism—In this type of interdependence, "two or more providers independently deliver the same services to the same market, but are either unaware of each other's activities or are unconcerned and are not deliberately reacting to or anticipating one another's actions" (p. 94). Two agencies in a large city offer similar literacy programs for adults. Since the number of potential learners far outstrips the capacity of the

two agencies, they work along side each other, unconcerned with the other's programming or marketing efforts.

3. Competition—In this case, " . . . two or more providers offer programs on a specific topic and aimed at a specific market, with full knowledge that others are doing the same, and react to or anticipate one another's initiatives" (p. 95). For example, two universities offer comparable master's degree programs in education within the same city, and being fully aware that each is doing so, develop marketing plans to compete for the same potential students.
4. Cooperation—This is a strategy in which providers assist each other on an ad hoc basis, for example, by providing mailing lists to each other or recommending instructors.
5. Coordination—In this type of interdependence, organizations ensure " . . . that their activities take into account those of other organizations on a consistent basis" (Lindsay, Queeney, & Smutz, 1981, p. 5). One university may focus its off-campus programming at the graduate level, leaving undergraduate programming to other institutions. In this way, the different institutions develop distinctive market niches and by taking each other into account avoid direct competition for the same set of learners.
6. Collaboration—This form of interdependence is the highest form. In this type, providers work " . . . together jointly and continuously on a particular project towards a specific goal" (Lindsay, Queeney, & Smutz, 1981, p. 5). The most common manifestation of collaboration is cosponsorship of programs.

Although Cervero noted that the orientations in this typology were distinct, Tallman (1990) found that the three forms of interorganizational relationships (cooperation, coordination, and collaboration) are not distinct. Rather, they exist on a continuum defined by the intensity of interactions among participating organizations. The more intense the interactions, the higher the type of interdependence. Tallman (1990) defined intensity as the amount of " . . . investment of each organization in the risks and benefits of the program, and the level of responsibility that each organization had in sponsoring it" (p. 151). Gray (1989) underscored Tallman's point, noting that level of intensity is related to the type of partnership formed among organizations.

While this book focuses on all three types of relationships (cooperation, coordination, and collaboration) in the planning and delivery of programs, its particular emphasis is on the highest form of interdependence, collaboration. This provision of programs is distinct from other types in the centrality joint decision making plays in the process. In collaboration, decisions do not concentrate solely on the programming itself. At least as important is their definition of the problem to be addressed through programming and the future of that problem as a consequence of the educational intervention provided. Although collaborators may have some idea in mind about the type of program needed to assist in resolving problems of child abuse, discussions among participants will contribute to new understandings and definitions of this problem. As a consequence, the design of the educational program for this problem domain (assuming an educational intervention is warranted) will be informed by the new understandings and definition of the problem gained through collaboration. In this book a problem domain is a situation, such as low literacy rates or teenage pregnancy, that two or more organizations may choose to address jointly through educational programming. Stakeholders are organizations and individuals who have a stake in the problem domain, its resolution and future. Bringing the appropriate stakeholders together to address the problem domain is an important component and skill in these efforts (Gray, 1989), a skill that is addressed more fully later in the section on leadership.

According to Gray (1989), the key characteristics of collaboration include the following:

- The solutions developed for the problem domain emerge as a result of organizations and individuals dealing constructively with their differences.

- Participating organizations and individuals assume joint ownership of the decisions reached to address the problem domain.
- The stakeholders assume collective responsibility for the future direction of the domain.
- The collaborative process itself is an emergent one (p. 227).

Both Cervero and Gray have cast collaboration into a political model in which the interests, costs, and benefits of potential partners have to be weighed as decisions are made and as arrangements emerge. In addition, Gray viewed "collaboration as [a] quasi-institutional mechanism for accommodating differing organizational interests" (p. 235). The "quasi-institutional" nature of collaborative relationships draws our attention to the organizational nature of these arrangements, as well as to the unconventional ways they are organized and governed.

COLLABORATIVE ARRANGEMENTS AS UNCONVENTIONAL ORGANIZATIONAL FORMS

Collaborative arrangements are a form of organization (Benson, 1975; Larson, 1992; Ring & Van de Ven, 1994; Thorelli, 1986). They are characterized by social structure (regularized aspects of the relationships existing among participants); participants who make contributions to the organization; goals; a technology, or way of doing work; and, their own environment (Scott, 1987). In addition, they have their own boundaries, and cultural and political issues abound within them. As organizations, however, they do have several special characteristics.

First, they are organizations formed by boundary spanning persons, or individuals who cross the boundaries of two or more organizations to create these new organizations. Second, these organizations are temporary. Although the length of time they exist varies, their "lifespan" generally is more limited than that of the partner organizations that support their development. Third, they are organizations formed by and between two or more *sovereign* and *distinct* organizations. The relationship that exists between the organizations in a collaborative arrangement is a "loosely coupled" one, meaning that through collaboration each partner simultaneously asserts its autonomy and distinctiveness *and* its interdependence on and responsiveness to the other organizations (Limerick & Cunnington, 1993; Orton & Weick, 1990). These seemingly contradictory elements of collaborative arrangements contribute much to the need for unconventional structures and means of governance.

Each new collaborative effort begins in an undifferentiated state, or "mess" (Gray, 1989). Issues of authority, role differentiation, control of work and activities, and values and norms are embedded in this mess and must be dealt with. Research has shown that, especially in informal collaborative arrangements, these issues are resolved through a variety of interpersonal and social processes. These processes lead to a negotiated order and to socially constructed meanings that are shared by participants (Gray, 1989; Larson, 1992). The negotiated order and socially constructed meanings contribute to the formation of psychological and social contracts (as opposed to legal ones) among participants that guide their work.

These psychological and social contracts have several important characteristics. First, in contrast to legal contracts that tend to be static, psychological and social contracts are dynamic (Gray, 1989). Order is constantly being negotiated and meanings are constantly changing as the developmental process that underlies collaboration proceeds. Second, the contracts are developed through mutual adjustment on the part of all participants. The contracts are also characterized by the presence of both implicit and explicit rules that guide the way participants work together. Fourth, control mechanisms are social. Social control is achieved both through individual, moral self-regulation, and through the joint determination of control mechanisms that establish expectations for others' behaviors (Larson, 1992). Fifth, psychological and social contracts are strengthened by the extent to which the reputation and identity of participating organizations and individuals are good and by the extent to which individual participants gain social satisfaction from participating in the collaborative arrangement.

Three additional and related factors are associated with the unconventional governance of collaborative arrangements: perceptions of fair dealing; development of transcendent values and norms; and open and honest communication among participants. For the development of a collaborative arrangement to proceed, all participants must believe that they are being dealt with fairly. Fair dealing requires equity, trust, and reciprocity (Ring & Van de Ven, 1994). In a collaborative arrangement it is not necessary that all risks and benefits be shared equally. Nonetheless, participants must believe that arrangements are equitable—that the benefits of their participation are proportional to their organization's investment (Ring & Van de Ven, 1994). Trust of others is also required, but it is a very fragile factor and takes time to build unless it exists prior to collaboration (Bergquist, Betwee, & Meuel, 1995; Gray, 1989; Larson, 1992). Participants must have trust in other partners' intentions, perspectives, competence, and capacities to fulfill their obligations (Bergquist, Betwee, & Meuel, 1995). This trust comes from the faith that the actions of others will be based on moral obligation and goodwill (Larson, 1992; Ring & Van de Ven, 1994). Ring and Van de Ven (1994) have noted that risk to trust, not economic risk, is the most important risk factor in collaborative arrangements. Reciprocity among participants is also required for a perception of fair dealing to exist. Reciprocity is a form of social indebtedness in which the obligation one has to another is diffuse and generalized. Reciprocity is often an unwritten rule in the social contract and results from initial exchanges among the parties to the collaboration (Larson, 1992; Ring & Van de Ven, 1994).

For collaboration to be successful it must also be characterized by the existence of transcendent values and norms. These include both the process norms of equity, trust, and reciprocity, but also shared values and norms that lead to a vision and goals for the collaborative effort. Gray (1989) has noted that these transcendent values arise from participants sharing responsibility for searching out information and sharing it with others, as well as from "joint appreciative processes." Appreciative processes are those in which participants come to appreciate individual and collective differences, perceptions, and appraisals of what is possible. Based upon these perceptions and appreciation of them, participants jointly make judgments of both fact and value related to an educational program. It is through these joint sharing and appreciative processes that meanings are socially constructed and a program vision developed.

Central to the processes described thus far is open and honest communication among all parties to the collaborative effort. Open, frequent, routine, and honest communication is necessary to foster fair dealing, to generate transcendent values, and to negotiate the order and social control required for the undertaking to succeed (Bergquist, Betwee, & Meuel, 1995). As will be noted in Chapters 4 and 5, tensions arising from these unconventional governance processes must be managed carefully for a relationship to be sustained. This requires a brand of leadership unique to collaboration.

LEADERSHIP IN COLLABORATIVE ARRANGEMENTS

The role of leadership in collaboration is much more complex than described in existing literature, and will be examined in greater detail in Chapter 3. First, we must consider the various leadership roles common to collaborative arrangements. As noted earlier, all involved parties are boundary-spanning persons in that they cross the boundaries of their respective organizations to work together. As they enter the process, they begin to assume roles, not as formally defined by their organization or by the collaborative arrangement, but informally as the social order is negotiated and socially constructed. The roles that individuals assume are based in part on other parties' perceptions of trust in the expertise, competence, and capacities of the individuals and the organizations they represent. Although many roles have been identified for participants, none is more important than leadership. Three major leadership roles have been identified in the literature—convener, product champion, and strategy maker. These three roles may be played by one person or several. In addition, different people may perform different roles as the arrangement proceeds through developmental stages and continues to evolve.

The convener (Gray, 1989; Larson, 1992) is the leadership role played by the person who identifies all the relevant stakeholders and brings them together to begin to address the problem domain. The product champion takes leadership in design and implementation by continually promoting the idea of collaborative programs and championing both the process and products of the project (Colgan, 1990). Effectiveness in this role is dependent upon the champion's ability to use personal relationships and informal mechanisms to achieve these ends (Cervero, 1992; Colgan, 1990).

The role of strategy maker is the closest parallel to leadership in the typical hierarchical authority structure of most organizations. The role is one of broker in which a series of roles is performed. Strategy makers serve as focal points for information, assume a position of centrality in the channeling of resources among partner organizations, as well as among and between individual participants, and mediate and resolve conflict (Lawless & Moore, 1989; Miles & Snow, 1986). Research has shown the strategy maker to be more influential in strategic decisions about the collaborative effort than individual managers in partner organizations and in cases where scarce resources are allocated to partner organizations (Lawless & Moore, 1989). The amount of effort the strategy maker must exert is dependent upon how evenly power is shared. The more evenly power is shared, the less effort is required of the strategy maker (Lawless & Moore, 1989).

DEVELOPMENTAL STAGES OF COLLABORATIVE RELATIONSHIPS

Developmental stages of collaborative relationships have been addressed by several authors (Bergquist, Betwee, & Meuel, 1995; Gray, 1985, 1989; Kanter, 1994; Larson, 1992; Ring & Van de Ven, 1994). All specify comparable, although not always

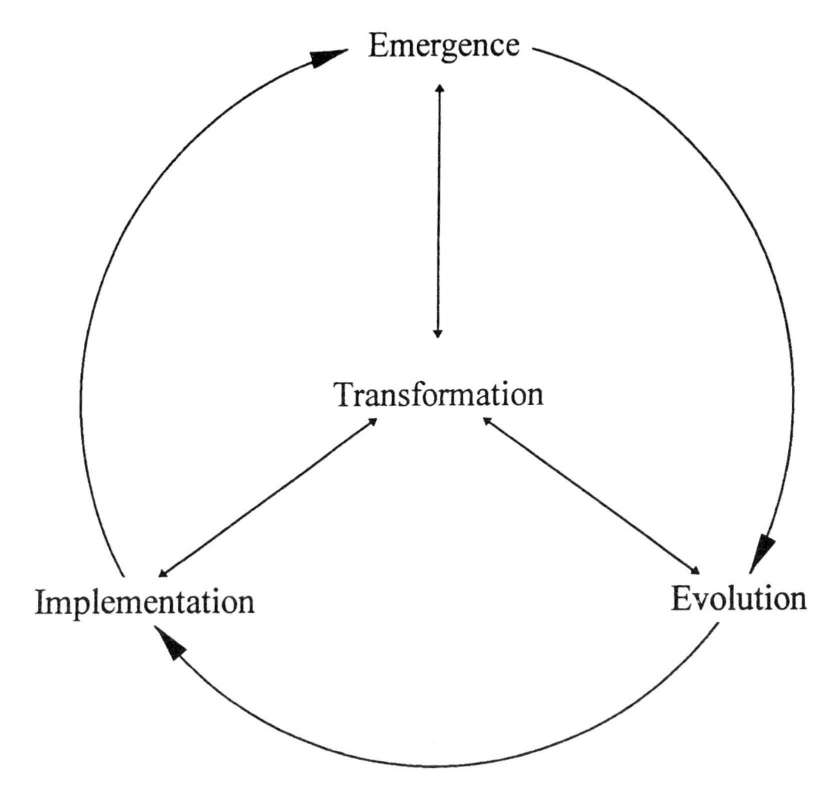

Figure 1.1. Developmental stages of collaborative relationships.

equivalent, characteristics or activities during stages, and several identify a different number of stages. A review of this literature has led to the identification of four stages in the life of a collaborative relationship: (a) emergence; (b) evolution; (c) implementation; (d) transformation. All stages are composed of different activities and processes. These relationships progress through the first three stages in order, although the length of time required for each varies and the boundaries among the stages are not always discrete. Transformation or change in relationships can occur at any stage of development and therefore is conceptualized as relating to and impacting each. (See Figure 1.1 for an illustration of these stages and their relation to transformation.) These four stages are described in the paragraphs that follow.

Emergence

Three major activities occur during the emergence stage: analyzing motives and reasons for collaborating and deciding to collaborate, identifying and selecting partners, and problem setting. Reasons for collaborating have been major areas of research and theory building for the past two decades. In a review of work in these areas, Oliver (1990) developed a typology of six motivating factors and reasons for organizations to collaborate:

- Necessity—The partnership is either mandated or required.
- Asymmetry—One organization enters the relationship to exercise power or control over another organization and its resources.
- Reciprocity—Organizations enter into the relationships for reasons of resource security; harmony, equity, and mutual support. In these cases, benefits are judged to exceed the costs of collaborating.
- Efficiency—Organizations collaborate to improve their input/output ratio.
- Stability—Organizations decide to collaborate in order to cope with and create predictability in their external environments.
- Legitimacy—Partnerships are seen as means to enhance an organization's credibility.

The adult education literature that addresses the topic of motives for collaborating focuses on all but the necessity and asymmetry factors identified by Oliver. For example, Beder (1978, 1984, 1987) developed an environmental interaction model of adult education agency cooperation that was based on four characteristics of adult and continuing education agencies—resource insecurity, need for flexibility (relative to environment), autonomy, and organizational insecurity. Beder noted that agencies cooperate to achieve vital ends that they cannot achieve alone, and to acquire resources (for example, money, learners, staff, information, work domain, and power) while avoiding constraints. For Beder, the benefits of collaborating should outweigh the costs (for example, time, goal displacement, lack of control).

Motivations and Incentives for Collaborating

The most extensive work in this area for adult education is Cervero's (1988, 1992) model of motivations and incentives for collaboration. Based upon the work of Schermerhorn (1975), this model conceptualizes collaboration as a political activity in which motivating factors, organizational and environmental influences, and potential costs work together to help the decision maker determine whether collaborating with another organization is a preferred action strategy. Cervero's model has been tested in research on adult education agencies (Colgan, 1990; Ferro, 1990; Tallman, 1990) and, with minor additions to the model, has been found to have good explanatory power about the decision to collaborate.

The model incorporates four variable categories: motivators; disincentives; organizational and environmental influences; and a cost-benefit dynamic. Incentives and motivators include organizational adversity, either resource scarcity or performance distress; positive valuing of collaboration, arising either within the organization or external to it; and external pressure to collaborate that comes from a powerful external source. Disincentives include loss of autonomy, image problems (for example, damage to prestige, identity, strategic position) that may arise from the collaborative effort, and the increased costs (for example, time, energy, direct costs of communication and transportation) associated with collaborating. Organizational and environmental influences include the organization's openness to its environment; mutuality in needs and purposes, complementary goals and the possibility for reciprocity among organizations; the opportunity and means (for example, geographic proximity, internal capacity) to collaborate; and the possibility of collaborating with the type of organization that the other organization prefers (Cervero, 1992; Ferro, 1990).

These three categories of variables are joined in a dynamic in which decision makers weigh costs and benefits in order to decide whether to collaborate. If no motivating condition is present, the decision maker would have no interest in collaborating. If at least one motivating condition is present but the decision maker perceives high potential costs or lack of organizational or environmental capacities, the provider might see the possibility of forming collaborative relationships but would not receive the extra push to view collaboration as a preferred action strategy. With the presence of at least one motivating condition, a low risk of incurring costs, and sufficient organizational and environmental capacities, the provider would seek out or be receptive to collaboration (Cervero, 1988, 1992).

While this model calls our attention to organizational incentives and motivations, others have also highlighted the individual value of collaboration (Tallman, 1990). Bergquist, Betwee, and Meuel (1995), as well as Kanter (1994), have noted that personal fulfillment and satisfaction also result from collaboration. Still others have identified a number of antecedent factors or preconditions that would predispose an organization to decide to collaborate. Larson (1992) has noted that good reputations of individuals in the other organization, histories of collaborative relationships, and good reputations of other organizations all predispose the decision maker to view collaboration favorably. These factors act in a way to reduce uncertainty, expectations and obligations, and enhance early cooperation. Therefore, the decision to collaborate is a complex activity affected by organizational, environmental, personal, and historical factors.

Identifying and Selecting Partners

Decisions to collaborate do not occur in the abstract. Rather, they occur in a real setting characterized by the existence of a real program, and a constellation of potential partners that present themselves to the decision maker at a particular point in time (Ferro, 1990). Therefore, deciding to collaborate is inextricably linked to identifying and selecting partners for the relationship. This identification process includes not only identifying potential partners that have similar interests and sufficient capacities to collaborate, but also analyzing the compatibility of the other organization(s) with one's own (Bergquist, Betwee, & Meuel, 1995; Kanter, 1994). Kanter has used the metaphor of courtship to describe this part of the collaborative process. It is a time of self-analysis and examining on the compatibility of other organizations with your own, and determining if the "chemistry" is there to support an "engagement" and possible "marriage."

Problem Setting

Once the decision has been made to collaborate and partners have been selected, the relationship begins to emerge through the process of problem setting (Gray, 1989). Problem-setting processes give the situation an explicit form or identity, allowing stakeholders to communicate about it and eventually act upon it (Gray, 1989). In essence, this activity involves the stakeholding partners arriving at a definition of the problem that they will address collaboratively. Three aspects of this activity are crucial. First, the stakeholders need to reflect on the complexity of the problem under consideration. Therefore, as partners are considered and selected, it is important to appraise whether organizations have a stake in the problem to be addressed. In addition, although there may be limits to the number of partners with which an organization can work, it should be remembered that from an information standpoint, the greater the number of stakeholders, the more effective the problem solution will be (Gray, 1985). Second, it is at this point that the convener leadership role is crucial. Problem setting is enhanced by conveners who possess legitimate authority and appreciative skills, and who can rally other stakeholders to participate (Gray, 1985). Third, in problem setting meanings begin to be socially constructed, order begins to be negotiated, and social and psychological contracts begin to be formed, as both explicit and implicit rules of the collaboration emerge (Larson, 1992; Ring & Van de Ven, 1994). During problem setting all the factors associated with these social processes introduced earlier (for example, trust, reciprocity, open and honest communications) play vital roles in getting the collaborative effort off to a good start and in establishing a foundation upon which the collaboration can build in later stages.

Ring and Van de Ven (1994) have posited that during the emergence stage, congruent sense making increases the likelihood of parties entering into formal negotiations about the collaborative effort. In essence, the more the parties to the collaboration see the problem congruently, the better the chances of the collaborative effort continuing into the next stages of development. They also have noted that congruent psychological contracts at this stage increase the likelihood of parties making a commitment to the collaborative effort. At this stage of collaboration, everything is informal. Therefore, the extent to which the parties get along and bond psychologically will have much to do with their commitment to continue in the effort.

The emergence stage of a collaborative interorganizational relationship is therefore a complex one, ranging from decisions to collaborate and with whom, to working together to define the problem to be addressed and to establish the social and psychological conditions for the effort's further development. If commitments are made to proceed during this stage, the collaboration moves into its next stage of development, evolution.

Evolution

Two interrelated activities are embedded in the evolution stage of the development. One of these, direction setting, involves making decisions about the purpose and direction of the effort. The other, although related to the first, focuses on issues associated with the maintenance and development of collaboration, in which integration and control are of central concern.

Direction Setting

In direction setting, " . . . stakeholders articulate the values that guide their individual pursuits and begin to identify and appreciate a sense of common purpose or direction" (Gray, 1989, p. 74). This purpose or the goals developed at this time generally are both strategic and operational. They spell out a vision for the collaborative effort, as well as some goals for how to get there (Larson, 1992). Collaboration is enhanced in direction setting when power is distributed among several rather than a few stakeholders. An equal power distribution is not necessary—it may actually create stalemate and inaction. But a sufficient power distribution is required to ensure that all stakeholders can influence decision making (Gray, 1985). Consequently, at this point in the development of the collaborative effort, the leadership roles of strategy maker and product champion take on increased significance, as the salience of the convener role diminishes.

Strength of jointly held beliefs and the development of values that transcend those of each organization also assist in direction setting. Joint information search can contribute to identifying transcendent values and jointly held goals for the temporary organization's work (Gray, 1985). Other fundamental ingredients for successful navigation of this developmental stage include respecting differences of opinion and culture; having frequent, open, and candid communications that focus on content (substance) as well as process; and, learning to collaborate by bridging differences through learning and through strategic, operational, tactical, interpersonal and cultural integration (Bergquist, Betwee, & Meuel, 1995; Kanter, 1994).

Maintenance and Growth

During the evolution stage participants begin to concentrate on the "glue" that will hold them together through this and future developmental stages. This glue is a complex mixture of maintaining trust, differentiating among the specialized functions each party to the collaboration will play, developing means for integrating these functions, and finding the appropriate balance between differentiation and integration (Bergquist, Betwee, & Meuel, 1995). In this case, integration is closely linked to social relations, which function to support coordination and control. For the collaboration to be maintained and grow during this stage, the factors associated with the unconventional forms of governance described earlier (for example, norms of fairness, honesty, reciprocity, and moral self-regulation) take on powerful roles, although they may remain invisible (Larson, 1992). In her study of successful collaborative efforts, Larson (1992) found that the moral control imposed was flexible yet pervasive. It prevented certain acts through the pressure of "its immediate regulatory presence" (Larson, 1992, p. 96), since behavior reflected on individual integrity and identity. Roles and identities became merged, resulting in self-regulation. These social patterns took on a rule-like status, in which patterned histories of interaction created mutual expectations that established the social contract and kept the collaborative effort growing (Larson, 1992; Meyer & Rowan, 1977).

From their observations of collaborative relationships, Ring and Van de Ven (1994) made the following comments about governance dynamics at this developmental stage: If the personnel in a collaborative arrangement remain the same, (a) personal relationships increasingly supplement role relationships as the collaboration develops over time; (b) informal psychological contracts increasingly compensate or substitute over time for formal contractual safeguards as reliance on trust among parties increases; and, (c) when the temporal duration of collaboration is expected to exceed the tenure of participating individuals, informal understandings and commitments will be formalized, probably in the form of a written contract. All three propositions point again to the importance of unconventional governance processes during this stage of development. As the last proposition indicates, the relationships and mutual adjustment that develop among individuals become so central to the functioning of the effort, that the specter of one or more individuals leaving may lead to formalization in order to protect remaining parties against the actions of potential newcomers

whom they have not yet learned to trust or who may have ideas that are contrary to the vision and direction that existing parties have identified.

Implementation

Implementation refers to engaging in actions necessary to realizing the vision and goals that were developed to deal with the problem domain (Gray, 1989)—simply put for the focus of this book, "offering the program." Successful implementation of programs is contingent upon the parties' collective ability to monitor and manage change in the temporary organization's external environment. This includes building relationships with outside actors, including other actors in the partnering organizations to insure agreements and actions are carried out; dealing effectively with other constituencies; building external support for the program; and monitoring the agreement and ensuring compliance with strategic, operational, and tactical goals. The implementation stage signals the fruition of all the collective efforts that have been invested up to this point. In some cases implementation draws collaboration to a close. In other cases, implementation of a program is but one point in a continuing effort concentrated around the offering of several programs over time. In still other cases, implementation and all that goes before it has established a history that becomes an antecedent condition to additional collaboration, either with the same organization(s) or others.

Transformation

Collaborative partnerships, like all organizations, are not immune to change. Rather, change is a constant in collaborative efforts, and as noted in the introduction to this section, may occur during any one of the other developmental stages. Change in a collaboration entails constant definition and redefinition of the relationship, constant re-creation, as opposed to stability (a hallmark of traditional, hierarchical organizations), and constant attention to the development of the scope and capabilities of the partnership (Bergquist, Betwee, & Meuel, 1995). Kanter (1994) has noted that change within collaborative efforts, especially change that contributes to their further growth, requires the development of an infrastructure for learning among the parties, as well as the empowerment of "relational" leaders like those described earlier who will champion the product and the unconventional processes by which these arrangements evolve. Such changes are generally of two types: redesign or termination (Bergquist, Betwee, & Meuel, 1995; Ring & Van de Ven, 1994).

Redesign

Redesign occurs for a number of reasons, including the addition or departure of partners or their individual representatives, changes in leadership and communication patterns, changes in the internal environments of partner organizations, and changes in the external environment, including in the market for the program offering. (Bergquist, Betwee, & Meuel, 1995). A few examples can illustrate changes that not only signal but call for further redesign of collaborative efforts:

- A partnership changes its name in order to reflect more accurately a change in its purposes and activities. A name change, however, has the potential for creating identity and image problems with external constituencies, requiring a redesign in the way collaborative parties have to work with these constituencies.
- A party to a collaborative effort is asked to leave because the organization did not live up to expectations, creating more difficulty than the benefits of having the organization participate. Asking the party to leave creates stress in and of itself, and remaining parties must renegotiate working relationships in a situation in which the social dynamics have changed.
- Members of a collaborative effort decide to change from face-to-face to distance education delivery for the programs they are sponsoring. Such a change has implications for the imple-

mentation stage of development, as well as potentially for the working arrangements and contracts (informal and/or formal) among parties.
- The balance of power among parties changes as a result of one organization suddenly having more access to money, leverage, and market. Again, such a change will put stress on the arrangement and will require a redesign of the social and formal contracts that have developed.
- A formal contract is written to institutionalize an arrangement that has developed informally. Formalization has the potential for disrupting informal working relationships since a formal contract may spell out roles and relationships that differ from those negotiated informally.

These examples illustrate the kinds of changes that can occur in collaboration. Each highlights the stresses created and the redesign necessary to sustain and further develop the relationship. Such changes also require flexibility on the part of participants and effective leadership in the redesign efforts that are required.

Termination

Termination is another form of change that is experienced in collaborative arrangements. In some cases, (for example, a short-term arrangement to cosponsor a program), termination is built into the collaborative effort from its inception. Once the program is implemented the collaboration simply ends. In other cases termination takes the form of the dissolution of a relationship that does not work. Again, a dissolution can occur at any of the other three stages. During emergence, parties may define the problem domain so differently that there is no reason to attempt further collaboration. In the evolution stage, any number of factors associated with the unconventional nature of collaborative governance may occur to trigger the demise of the collaboration. In the implementation stage, failure to adjust to changing environmental conditions, to enlist the support of constituencies, or to obtain sufficient external support may signal the fragility of the relationship and its potential end.

Research suggests four major events or factors that increase the potential for a relationship to end prematurely. The first of these is an imbalance in the formal/informal processes employed (Ring & Van de Ven, 1994). A move to more formality may occur, for example, as a result of bringing in specialized professionals (such as attorneys) who exhibit role-specific and rule-governed behavior that threatens the social and psychological contracts of participants. Second, change in personnel and/or in leadership leads to stress that may also threaten the collaboration. This type of change will be especially stressful if it also contributes to an imbalance in the collaboration's informal/formal processes. Lack of clarity in roles and relationships can also threaten a relationship. If the differentiation and integration that have resulted from social processes are disrupted, either by external changes or by participants acting in ways that diminish perceptions of trust and fair dealing, then the foundations upon which the relationship has developed are threatened. Finally, stress can occur by the partnership simply growing too big. Physical growth interferes with the spirit of community experienced by a smaller group of participants and also generates the need for more formality to ensure the smooth operation of the collaborative effort. Both contribute to fragility in the relationship, which if not managed effectively, can lead to the effort's demise (Bergquist, Betwee, & Meuel, 1995; Ring & Van de Ven, 1994).

Irrespective of the factors that lead to fragility and the potential end of a collaborative arrangement, there is one symptom that all fragile relationships exhibit—a decline in direct communication among participants (Bergquist, Betwee, & Meuel, 1995). This decline in both the quantity and quality of communication among parties signals a number of possibilities, foremost of which is that perceptions of trust and fair dealing have decreased. If such a symptom presents itself, it is insufficient to deal with the symptom. Rather, participants, particularly those playing leadership roles, must identify and deal with the root cause if the collaborative effort is to proceed.

When presented with the dilemma of a fragile relationship, a decision must be made about whether it is worth salvaging or whether actions should be taken to end it as gracefully as possible. Insights from informants presented in the following chapters provide some useful ways to think about this dilemma. Unfortunately, at times participants must deal with another kind of relationship—one that does not work and will not end. Circumstances beyond those related directly to the reasons to collaborate in the first place have come into play that prevent the effort from ending, although it would be best for all parties if it did. In general, as the temporal duration of a partnership increases, the chance of a dissolution tends to decrease. Length of time in collaboration leads to the development of very strong psychological and social contracts that work against termination. Likewise, the longer the collaboration the greater the odds that a formal legal contract has been exercised, binding the parties together even under circumstances that are less than healthy (Ring & Van de Ven, 1994). Extricating oneself and one's organization from these types of situations is particularly problematic. It requires sensitivity on the part of participants to the need to terminate a relationship when it lacks further instrumental value, even though it may still meet their social and psychological needs. This situation also requires participants to be willing to develop and renegotiate legal contracts that provide an escape clause permitting termination when the parties agree that the collaboration either is no longer effective or no longer serves the interests of partner organizations.

TENSIONS AND BALANCES

Embedded in the above discussion of the developmental stages of collaborative relationships is an implicit focus on the need for balance between formal and informal mechanisms. This balance is needed to ensure the maintenance and foster the development of collaborative relationships (Ring & Van de Ven, 1994). Ring and Van de Ven have highlighted the need for this balance for each of four different developmental processes inherent in a collaborative arrangement. For the process of negotiation, there is a need for balance between formal bargaining

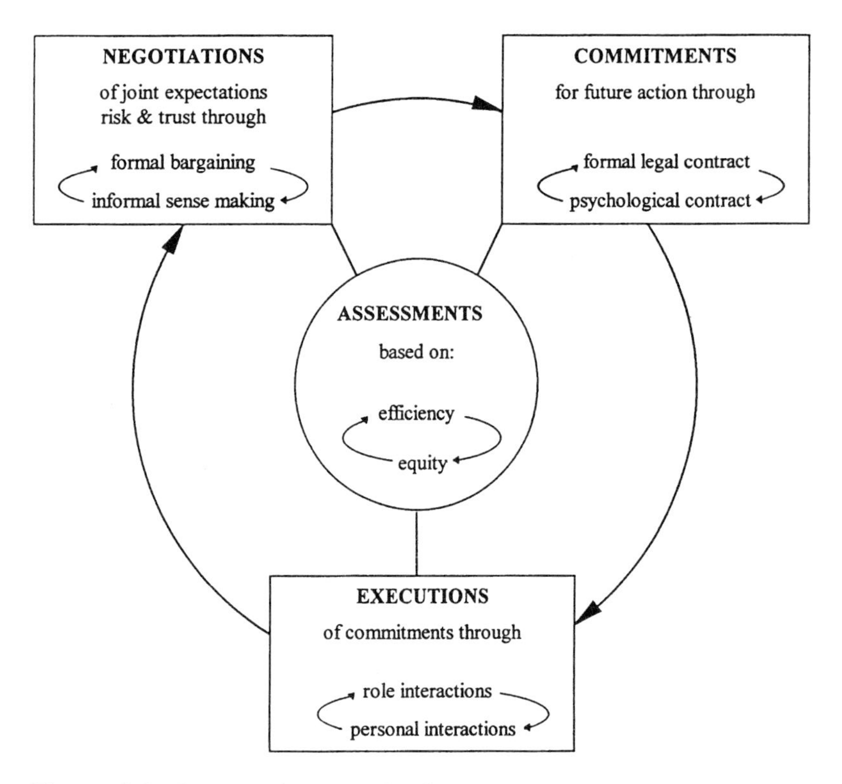

Figure 1.2. Process framework of the development of cooperative IORs (Interorganizational Relationships). *Note.* From "Developmental Processes of Cooperative Interorganizational Relationships," by P. S. Ring and A. H. Van de Ven, 1994, *Academy of Management Review, 19,* p. 97. Copyright by Academy of Management. Reprinted with permission.

and the informal sense making required to develop social and psychological contracts. For the process of making commitments, there must be a balance between formal legal contracts and informal, psychological and social ones. In executing agreements, there must be a balance between role interactions and personal interactions. In assessing the value of products and processes, efficiency (the least expensive way of getting things done) must be balanced against equity. (See Figure 1.2.)

Although the weight of discussion in this chapter has been

on the unconventional and social nature of collaborative structures and governance processes, work still must be accomplished, and this necessity focuses our attention on instrumental factors, such as efficiency, role behavior, formalization of agreements, and bargaining. But balance between the two extremes of formality and informality is crucial. Imbalance in the direction of formality leads to efficiency but may undercut the relational nature of collaboration and the social foundation required to get work done. Imbalance in the direction of informality contributes to effectiveness in relationship and vision building but may create inefficiencies in realizing the vision. The proper balance between these two extremes will vary for each situation. Insights from informants add to our understanding about how the proper balance can be achieved under differing circumstances.

CONCLUSION

This chapter has provided a summary of the literature on interorganizational relationships for the planning and delivery of educational programs for adults. In developing the summary, we drew on the general literature of organizational theory, as well as from the adult and continuing education literature that deals specifically with this topic. The unconventional, social, relational, and developmental nature of collaboration was emphasized, but balance between formality and informality also appears to be a prerequisite to effective efforts. We turn our attention now to considering how these ideas find expression in practice, as we consider collaboration from the perspective of adult and continuing educators involved in collaborative program activities in real settings.

CHAPTER 2

Linking Theory and Practice

In this chapter we describe the processes we used to select practitioners to interview, to gather information from them, and to analyze the information they shared. We also present brief descriptions of the practice settings in which these practitioners work. We furnish these descriptions for two reasons. First, they provide a backdrop and grounding for the practitioners' rich insights and experiences, which will be drawn upon in remaining chapters. Second, the practitioners' different settings affected the manner in which they addressed the various issues and tensions of collaboration. Closer examination of these settings in later chapters will reveal how they impact collaboration.

This chapter is, therefore, a transitional one. It provides a transition from the world of theory into the world of practice. But it does so in a way that connects the theory with the practice of collaboration, by highlighting interconnecting themes of practice and theory and grounding the practice of collaboration within a variety of adult and continuing education practice settings.

THE ADULT AND CONTINUING EDUCATION PRACTITIONERS AND THEIR ROLE AS INFORMANTS

Eight adult and continuing education practitioners, representing seven different practice settings across the United States, agreed to participate with us in gaining a deeper and richer understanding of collaboration among organizations in the planning and delivery of educational programs. For the purposes of this book, we have chosen to call these practitioners "informants." We have selected this label to emphasize the valuable role that such individuals play in contributing to thorough understanding of the meaning and social dynamics that are embedded in specific social and cultural contexts.

The informants for this book shared five very important characteristics:

- A deep and thorough knowledge of the situations they described
- A great deal of practical experience with both successful and unsuccessful collaborative efforts
- An ability to reflect on experience and to make explicit the details and nuances of those experiences that an outside observer might overlook
- Skill in communicating so that those unfamiliar with their situations could easily understand them
- Patience to explain fully in response to the questions asked

The informants were identified by first listing the several areas of adult and continuing education practice that should be represented in the book. Our goal was to have as large a range in settings as feasible. Then, lists of prominent individuals in each area were developed, using recommendations from several adult and continuing education colleagues. Once individuals were identified, they were contacted and asked to participate in providing information for this book. Each informant agreed to participate in a series of in-depth interviews and provide us with documentation about their organizations and collaborative efforts.

Informants were ensured anonymity and confidentiality so that they would be willing to share both their successful and unsuccessful experiences in working with others. We quickly came to appreciate the wealth of experience they have had with collaborative efforts, the practical wisdom and important insights they have developed in that experience, and the value of their contributions to this project.

Using the material in Chapter 1, we developed a list of

questions designed to elicit comments about each informant's experiences with collaboration. These questions were pilot tested with two other individuals, who, because of their roles in planning and managing adult and continuing education programs, could also have been informants. Copies of the questions asked are found in the Appendix. We also provided informants with early drafts of the Preface, Chapter 1 and this chapter. We shared these earlier drafts to help informants see how theoretical perspectives drawn from a variety of disciplines influenced the questions we asked, and to help them gain an accurate understanding of the purposes and approaches we were taking in writing this book.

Although we asked informants specific questions, we did so in a way that permitted them to go beyond our questions, addressing topics that they believed were essential to understanding collaboration in their settings. In most cases, we also asked them a second set of questions to broaden the information and obtain details on specific situations and issues they had introduced in earlier responses. As a result, they provided us with rich case examples and a wealth of insights and observations that added detail to theory and brought it to life. All interviews were tape recorded and distilled into extensive notes by each author. We also compared our independent analyses to ensure that our interpretations were consistent and accurate. Finally, we checked our analyses with selected informants to ensure that our interpretations accurately represented the meanings they were communicating. In our estimation, informants' participation in this project was invaluable. We trust that you will also conclude that their contributions were indispensable to gaining deeper understandings of collaboration in adult and continuing education practice.

THE PRACTICE SETTINGS

Seven practice settings were selected for study. With the help of informants, we prepared the following general descriptions of the settings and the educational programs offered within each.

Park District

This park district is located in a city of 150,000, with a highly diversified local economy and population. The city's economic base is further characterized by the presence of a large number of high technology and service companies and very little heavy industry. The median income is $35,000 and a higher than average proportion of the population has college degrees. The school system remains reasonably sound, but faces financial pressure because of increased enrollments at the elementary level. There is a great deal of support in the city for recreation programs for all age groups. As evidence of this support, many citizens have donated land, buildings, and money to help build a comprehensive system of parks and support recreational programs sponsored by the district.

The park district catalog is nearly 100 pages long. Programs offered include sports leagues, fitness and health activities, educational programs for citizens ranging from children to older adults, and a wide variety of special events. What is notable about the district's programs is the large number that are cosponsored and/or supported by public and private organizations in the community.

The park district's director has lived in the community for nearly 30 years and is locally and nationally respected. Programs offered by the district often receive national awards for excellence. The director collaborates as easily as he breathes and has established a culture within his organization that promotes the development of collaborative programs. The district's success in obtaining grants, financial and other gifts, and community support via property tax increases is evidence of how successful it has been in building support through collaboration.

Professional Association

This association began when North American research and industry scientists decided that standard measurement methods were needed in their laboratories. Eventually the association added publications and educational programs as its membership grew to over 1,000 by the early 1940s. Membership dropped below 1,000 in the early 1970s due to constriction in employment opportunities for members of the profession. At this time the association began to explore ways to expand its membership and scope of influence beyond North America. It exported programs to western Europe and experienced an almost immediate spike in European membership and in European scientists' participation in programs offered in North America. The association has continued to develop internationally, focusing on program offerings and membership recruitment in Central and South America, Africa, Southeast Asia, and eastern Europe. As a result, non-North American membership has grown to nearly 40 percent of the total, which also has more than doubled. More recently, the association has looked to "fringe" areas of interest to attract new members and develop new programs.

The approaches used to increase membership and expand influence have included complex collaborative relationships with related associations (including non-North American ones), governmental agencies, and multinational companies whose global interests could be served through the association's international efforts. Collaboration has been successful because the association has been careful to invite other associations to participate as equals and because it is very aware of the need for sensitivity to cultural and political diversity.

Educational Program for Local Government Officials

This program resides at a major land-grant university and has been in operation for 18 years. It is a joint effort of two units with major responsibility for outreach at the institution. Major funding for the program came through grants from a national foundation and a few local ones. The focus of the program has been to increase the capacity of county, municipal and township officials in large rural areas of this state to make sound decisions.

All of the educational and service efforts of the program

have a number of cosponsors. They include academic units at the land-grant university, state governmental agencies, professional associations for local government officials, the state's other higher education institutions, and not-for-profit organizations. The program provides the administrative support, marketing and financial management for each activity. Cosponsors have expertise in specialized topics, including financial management, personnel management, solid and hazardous waste disposal, economic development, general management issues, and public health, among others. Activities, services and publications produced by the program are planned jointly, with other cosponsors and local government officials. The program has relied a great deal on technology to deliver programs to sites close to where local government officials live. This strategy has been effective, as has attention to the timeliness of issues addressed, the brevity of programs, and preparation of clearly written explanatory materials.

The program has always been willing to collaborate with other organizations interested in working with local government officials. Its guiding philosophy has been to collaborate rather than compete. Collaboration has not always been possible, because there are many providers of education and services for local government officials, some of whom do not believe that collaboration is in their best interest. As the program has matured, it has broadened to include applied research efforts, policy analysis work, and events on specialized topics such as welfare reform, rural poverty and developing elder-friendly rural communities. There also have been efforts to assist communities in times of crises, such as during floods and droughts.

Consulting Firm

This consulting firm provides several different types of educational and organizational development programs and services to a range of for-profit and not-for-profit organizations. However, it also functions in a unique fashion for a consulting firm in that it also collaborates with other organizations (for example, state and local governments, professional associations, institutions of higher education) to provide its various services. The firm employs several professional staff members with a range of expertise in organizational studies and education. In addition, the services and programming offered by this firm are informed and guided by principles of adult and continuing education and a commitment to collaborate with others whenever possible.

The specific experience that was shared by the representative of this consulting firm relates to a long-term collaborative arrangement that the firm has had with a governmental agency. As part of this arrangement, the consulting firm also collaborates with several professional associations that are informally and loosely affiliated with the agency. The focus of this collaboration has been on developing and offering a range of educational programs that serve agency staff, the individuals and groups the agency serves, and members of the affiliated professional associations. The firm's ability to collaborate is based both on its stance toward collaboration and its reputation for repeated success in planning and offering continuing education programs in collaboration with others. The firm's experience with the long-term collaborative arrangement provides many insights about how these undertakings can change and evolve over time.

Distance Education Consortium

This distance education consortium is directed by one of our informants. However, his major role is to direct a university continuing education unit that is well known for its pioneering use of distance education methods in programming for adults. His university, through the office of continuing education, participates in this voluntary statewide distance education consortium with the state's other institutions of higher education. The purpose of this consortium is to offer a coordinated set of educational offerings to the state's adult population, especially in rural areas, where educational needs are particularly diverse.

This collaborative effort is a form of cooperation, since the consortium provides a means for competing institutions to take each other into account in their programming, develop unique market niches, and through coordinated effort better serve citizens through use of telecommunications technologies.

The distance education consortium exists within another collaborative arrangement mandated by state legislation. Purposes of this mandated arrangement are the development and maintenance of an extensive telecommunications network in order to make educational programs accessible to the state's population. The distance education consortium was formed in part to provide more coordinated programming, but also to address concerns about the potential erosion of state support for the network unless increased levels of educational benefit could be demonstrated to lawmakers. The consortium is making progress in the development of courses and degree programs, and has recently secured state funding for staffing its day-to-day operations.

Staff Development Organization for Educators

This private, not-for-profit staff development organization for educators is dedicated to systemic change of education. It collaborates with a range of educational and community organizations and stakeholders to help educators rethink and reexamine their practice, and utilizes a range of programming approaches to fulfill this mission.

This organization has a rich history in collaborating with others. In fact, collaboration is a major means through which it develops and offers its programs, and the importance of collaboration permeates the organization's culture and the professional development of its staff. The organization has been very successful in attracting grant and gift support for its programs, owing, in part, to the success that it has demonstrated in collaborating with a range of other organizations (for example, businesses, not-for-profit agencies, government entities, schools and school districts, universities, foundations) to address effectively a range of complex problems confronting this nation's educational systems.

University Graduate Department

This university department is located at a major research institution. It has recently been collaborating with six other state institutions of higher education to develop and offer a statewide, cooperative, cohort graduate program to a group of professionals located throughout the state. Although the graduate degree is offered by the research university and is governed by the university's graduate policies, comparable departments, administrators, and faculty members at all partner institutions participate in developing program policy, reviewing and admitting students, developing the program's curriculum, and teaching courses. The collaborative relationship is governed by a council of deans and a coordinating committee composed of department heads and other faculty. These bodies are chaired respectively by the research university's dean and department chair. Other means have been used, however, to extend participation in the partnership to faculty members at all participating institutions. Faculty members have participated in large meetings devoted to developing the program's curriculum, and teams composed of faculty members from participating institutions develop and teach most courses offered in the program.

State funding has been obtained to support the program, and resources from this funding have been shared among participating institutions to fund new faculty positions and support the program in other ways. Distance education technologies are used to connect students and instructors during fall and spring semesters, when students take courses at participating institutions. All students are brought together on the research university's campus during two summers, at which time a team of faculty members from participating institutions delivers instruction during an intense four-week summer session. The continuing education office, located in the research university's participating college, has also contributed to the effort, especially in support of the summer instructional program, part of which is also delivered off-campus through face-to-face instruction and distance education technologies.

CONCLUSION

The only characteristics these informants share are active involvement in developing adult and continuing education programs and rich experience in using collaboration to do so. But although their approaches to collaboration have some major similarities, we will find that they differ in some very important ways. To illustrate both the agreement and difference between the various approaches, we begin with the informants' experience with leadership and vision—roles which together form a major theme in the theory and practice of collaboration.

CHAPTER 3

The Roles of Leadership and Vision

We begin this chapter with a hypothetical example drawn from informant comments to demonstrate several aspects of leadership in collaborative program planning. In this example, the director of a community adult education program wants to initiate a literacy-welfare to work program. She had seen the results of similar efforts on a visit to a city in another state and, despite the differences, could picture how this program would work in her community. "I could see in my mind's eye how the cosponsors would have to work together, some of the possible bumps in the road, and how all of us could win through being involved."

The director believed that her leadership would be necessary throughout this new program's development. She personally visited potential cosponsors and recruited influential individuals to serve on the steering committee. Equally important, the director communicated her enthusiasm for the new program, especially during the early planning stages. What made her so enthusiastic was the connection between literacy training and the possible transition from welfare to work with a future. She especially wanted to involve those in the community whom the adult education program had not reached in the past.

Given her enthusiasm for this new program and its potential, she made a commitment to remain the program's leader through the planning period and until a strong foundation had been developed for it. This commitment was unusual, since she tended to stay in the background, and promote her staff's participation in collaborative ventures, or contribute to them as a committee member or advisor when needed.

Her experience points out two elements important to successful collaboration—the critical roles of leadership, and a vision that drives the development of new programs. In this chapter, we will examine the following topics related to leadership and vision:

- The varied leadership roles that are required in collaboration
- The challenges that leaders face in collaboration
- The common characteristics of effective leadership in collaborative efforts
- The necessity for a vision, and its role in motivating and guiding leadership performance

LEADERSHIP ROLES

In Chapter 1, three major leadership roles were identified—convener, champion, and strategy maker. As our informants emphasized, they all played different and significant leadership roles when a collaborative activity began and as it continued to develop. They also added important dimensions to our understanding of the three major leadership roles identified in the literature. For the convener and strategy maker roles, these dimensions led to identification of several subroles that contributed to effective performance of the major one. We have chosen to label these subroles with short descriptors, followed by a description of each.

Convener

Persons playing the convener leadership role identify and bring together a set of stakeholders to address a problematic situation through educational programming. The example provided at the beginning of this chapter is illustrative. The adult education program director sought to bring together stakeholders to address the community problem of illiteracy through collaborative programming. But, as the example also illustrates, the program director first identified an opportunity for programming in this area. She also purposefully chose to remain personally involved and visible in providing leadership for the effort. Her performance highlights three subroles that contributed to her performance as a convener—initiating collaborative programming, building a supportive alliance, and being visible or invisible when convening stakeholders, depending upon a variety of situational factors.

Initiator

Initiators see collaborative program opportunities that will be of value to their organizations and the learners they currently serve or may serve. These opportunities present themselves as new program topics or different groups of potential participants. This leadership role is like the entrepreneurial role in business. Initiators do not wait for opportunities to occur but are continually looking for them and exploring how program ideas might become realities. Never complacent, they look for unfilled niches. They have a network of colleagues and clients who provide information and guidance about opportunities. They study similar settings or organizations to learn what might work in their own settings and for their own organizations. When opportunities are identified, they act to bring together stakeholders to capitalize on them.

Alliance Builder

In the alliance builder role, persons place themselves at the center of activity and orchestrate the building of alliances among groups that do not normally work together. As in the case of the adult education program director, her image and standing in the community made her very able to perform this role. She brought together groups from the public and private sectors to plan and support her program idea, relying on individuals and businesses to provide financial and other forms of support.

All informants described in detail how many people are

part of their networks, and how much time is spent gathering information from others. They emphasized that alliances had to be built and maintained, although these alliances may not be relied upon in each programming situation. A broad range of alliances was therefore maintained by these practitioners, from which they could draw when particular program initiatives required the collaboration of specific stakeholders. The park district manager worked closely and continually with the leaders in public schools, social service organizations, health care systems, and the general business community. The association director paid particular attention to associations that could be collaborators, as well as to trade groups that often provided financial support for educational programs. The local government education director and his staff developed advisory groups to expand the program's network of relationships. The staff development organization informants maintained close ties with a wide variety of agencies and associations. For example, they noted that, "For the type of programs that we do to succeed, we must be able to get help from many of the agencies that receive some funding from the United Way," highlighting the breadth of organizational types with which they continually worked to support systemic change, the focus of much of their collaborative programming.

As alliance builders, leaders also create conditions which allow groups to compromise and work together. Again the reputation and standing of the leader make this possible. The reputation of alliance builders is enhanced when other stakeholders clearly see alliance builders as persons whose intent is to develop programs that benefit everyone rather than promote their own personal interests or that of their organizations.

Behind the Scenes Orchestrator

In the example of the community adult education program director, a decision was made to be visible in convening the group of stakeholders to collaborate on the literacy program. However, being visible is not always necessary or prudent. For a variety of reasons, a person may wish to remain in the background and work with others to orchestrate the initiation and development of a collaborative effort. Why? The answer may be a simple one, such as a lack of time. A second reason could be interest in giving a colleague the opportunity to perform a visible leadership role. Or, the person may not want to be seen as playing a major role in order to avoid difficulties associated with working with others with whom there is a history of conflict.

Both the association director and the park district manager identified situations in which they stayed behind the scenes at the start. In the former's case, initial negotiations were held between the association's president and the head of another association as the first step in planning a joint program. "They both are scientists; I am not," the director said. "My president felt there were issues best discussed alone, before the full group got together." The park district manager recounted several instances in which he assumed a "behind the scenes" stance, supporting staff members in playing the convener role, but staying informed of progress so that he could provide help as needed.

Champion

Information gathered from informants indicated that the role of champion was particularly important in the emergence stage of a collaborative relationship's development, when support for the program idea and opportunity must be developed. But, this role was also important in other developmental stages, both in keeping the collaborative process moving along and in helping collaborators maneuver through difficulties.

Individuals take on the mantle of a champion for the program idea, promoting it to both internal and external stakeholders, thereby moving the idea forward for further investigation and possible development. This leadership role involves testing the idea among colleagues, obtaining approval to go ahead from senior management, and sounding out representatives of other groups to determine their interest level. The person who plays this leadership role also may begin to gather information to support the idea, including identifying where similar programs have been offered and with what success, what groups cosponsored the program elsewhere, and how much money was required to present the program.

As information is gathered, the leader may become more or less enthusiastic about the idea. One informant indicated that he had abandoned a number of attractive ideas after the amount of time and money involved was determined, thereby choosing not to champion them. A second informant, who heads a local government training program, indicated that he used a "test" of appropriateness and "need to know" when evaluating possible new programs and their value to an audience of part-time local government officials. As an example, he cited a leadership development program with the largest local government association in the state. "We spent a lot of time listening to very knowledgeable, credible people in the association as we shaped the idea for the program. That way, association representatives and leaders became as enthusiastic about the program as we were, and sold the program idea to their membership."

Through this information and opinion gathering, the leader strengthens his or her position in playing the role of champion. Strong and confident advocacy is more likely. With facts and figures, recommendations will be received with greater respect. A better decision on next steps is certainly a likely result.

Informants were not only champions at the beginning of collaborative efforts. They also maintained this leadership role through further developmental stages. A central strategy they used in performing this role was to ensure that both small and large successes of the effort were celebrated by collaborators and communicated to other important leaders and stakeholders in partner organizations, in other organizations, and in the community. By ensuring that these successes were recognized, they maintained and built support internally and externally for the effort, increased enthusiasm for progress being made, and enhanced collaborators' motivations for continuing to work together toward achievement of their jointly developed vision. The strategy of recognizing small successes was particularly important when the collaborative relationship was experiencing stress due to internal or external forces. The recognition of progress made and the celebration of achieving milestones often reduced stress sufficiently and increased motivation enough to allow partners to work through difficult times.

Therefore, the leadership role of champion is an important one. It contributes to moving program ideas into consideration by a range of stakeholders, and it helps sustain relationships and get them through difficult times.

Strategy Maker

As noted in Chapter 1, the role of strategy maker is a composite of leadership behaviors in which the leader channels and manages resources, deals with power dynamics, and assists the partnership in getting its work done. Informants did not mention the strategy maker role directly, but all were involved in performing it. They managed financial resources and budgets, helped divide and coordinate tasks, developed and monitored time lines for work to be completed, ensured that evaluation reports were developed and submitted on time, helped partners realize when they had reached milestones, and dealt with conflicts resulting from different interests and power balances within the group. They also identified several other leadership behaviors that contribute to the performance of the strategy maker role. These included the subroles of "wary innovator," "negotiator," "pacesetter," "critic," and "blocker."

Wary Innovator

Informants were "wary innovators," cautiously assessing if a project was worth their organization's time and interest, especially when new projects were being considered. Of particular concern was the amount of effort required to work with the potential group of cosponsors, the political risks, and the possible payoffs. As one informant pointed out: "Sometimes no real decision is required, because all of the groups have worked together in the past. However, adding just one new organization can change the chemistry and we will look long and hard before inviting in a new partner." This example highlights the way informants were "wary" as they considered entering a collaborative arrangement.

In contrast, informants from the staff development organization provided an example of "wariness" once collaboration had begun: "We can never get too far ahead of our colleagues. Our role is to broker and bring people together to plan. Their ideas guide the directions we take." Caution in this instance related to how directive leaders should be in guiding the group in developing its vision. The local government program was faced with the challenge of overcoming resistence to mediated instruction. As a result, audio and then video teleconferencing were very slowly added as delivery mechanisms for programs, as support for these forms of delivery was garnered over time from partner organizations. In these two cases, the strategy was to defer to the group as decisions were made. However, as will be illustrated in descriptions of other leadership roles, a more proactive strategy is at times required.

This role brings into relief informants' consideration of the relationship between innovation and risk, for their own organizations as they considered collaborating, and for both the partnerships and their own organizations, once collaboration began. Their attention to both innovation and risk influenced the strategy they selected and employed through all developmental stages of collaboration. As will be noted in a later section, informants also identified a variety of risks, including image and political ones, that challenged their performance of leadership roles. In addition, a theme introduced in the next chapter, the tension between risk taking and risk avoidance, draws our attention to risks to fair dealing (trust, equity, and reciprocity) within collaborative relationships. Thus, this leadership role highlights the relationship between leading and taking risks within collaboration. It also accentuates the intensity with which a variety of risks are monitored and the caution required in taking risks as leadership roles (especially the strategy maker role) are performed.

Negotiator

As a subset of the strategy maker role, the leader also will negotiate with cosponsors to ensure that a new or established program is moving forward in logical directions. In the cases of the association director and the park district manager, they made scientists from around the world and citizens from a single local community understand what could be done with the finances that were available. In other instances, the park district manager concentrated on the mix of elements in a program, and suggested which ones might be eliminated or reshaped. Given his standing and reputation in the community, he was able to negotiate with individuals and the entire committee to achieve the results he desired. Negotiations may also include suggesting that a program effort be smaller rather than larger. This applied particularly to the park district manager who believed that a successful small program would be better than a large and complicated one that never took place.

The negotiator role was also evident in the development of formal agreements among participating organizations. Responsibilities for financial risks and gains were specified, and the roles and responsibilities of each participating organization were stipulated. As will be seen in the next chapter, informants either preferred to avoid formal negotiation or to make negotiation as simple and straightforward as possible. Most believed that complex negotiations tended to get in the way of relationship building and program planning. For this reason, they preferred the informal processes of sense making, consensus, and mutual accountability to gain commitment, divide and execute tasks, and monitor and assess the relationship and its work. Yet, when necessitated by situational and organizational factors, they readily engaged in negotiating as part of their strategy maker role.

Pacesetter

The skilled leader uses experience as a guide to know just how fast the collaborative effort should move. Informants offered mixed opinions about this role. Some believed that they should be in charge of pacing at all times. Others let the group govern speed, so that all participating organizations were comfortable with the rate at which program direction was solidified and the speed with which the program was developed. The pace of work is therefore an element of collaborative work that must be addressed by strategy makers. They can attempt to control the pace of work themselves or they may choose to defer to the group to establish its own pace for getting work done. Who controls the pace of work appears to be both a function of personal preference and the progress of the collaborative effort. Some informants noted, for example, that while they preferred to let the group choose its own pace, they were not averse to intervening if deadlines were not being met or if the pace of work appeared too slow for the group to meet its various milestones.

Critic

Criticism is needed at different times in all collaborative arrangements in order to assess the direction being taken, the progress being made, the processes being used, or the quality of the relationship itself. Persons can play the role of critic directly with the entire group or by consulting with individuals outside of meetings. Several of our informants recounted experiences in which they performed this role in these two ways. They also highlighted the importance of the relationship between the experience and stature of the person who wishes to play this role and his or her acceptability and efficacy in performing it. It appears that credibility, past successful experiences in collaboration, and a reputation for fair dealing all contribute to group members accepting the criticism offered by a person. However, the climate of the group also may either support or interfere with needed criticism. For example, the distance education consortium was made up of competitors who were taking each others' programming into account through coordinative processes. By virtue of this type of collaborative arrangement and the fact that it existed within the context of another mandated relationship, criticism appeared to be suppressed rather than encouraged. The effective performance of this role is therefore very much a function of the person and the climate of the group.

Blocker

At times, the leader will act as a blocker. This is a very important role as a collaborative effort begins but is a particularly sensitive role and usually is performed circumspectly. If a project takes a potentially harmful direction, the blocker may try to halt progress until the reasons for and the consequences of that direction can be fully explored. Again, we found our informants using experience as a guide in helping them decide when and if to perform this strategic role.

Although the leader may need to slow planning to ensure that a variety of issues are addressed before progress is resumed, the blocker role may also require the halting or dissolution of a collaboration. For example, the park district manager worked to end a community program when he felt that support for it from the local business community was waning. He also reported an instance in which he believed that the planning for a new program was so shaky that the effort ought to be abandoned. According to him, "the rest of the group was waiting for someone to take the leadership and do what I did." So, to the relief of other participants, he performed the role of blocker and suggested that the undertaking be dissolved. In another case, the professional association director worked vigorously to prevent programs from being held in one specific foreign country because of previous unpleasant experiences arranging meetings there. In the local government education program, part-time elected officials often performed this leadership role. They tended to distrust information that came from sources outside their area of the state. As a result, they slowed the group's deliberation until they were convinced that the information had relevance for them and others in similar situations.

The blocker role contributes to strategy in two ways. By slowing progress, the group is forced to deal with and resolve important strategic issues directly and candidly before moving on. By leading efforts to dissolve the relationship, blockers act to reduce costs to their and other organizations. Ending an unproductive relationship before feelings are hurt also has the strategic advantage of preserving the possibility for working together again when success is more likely.

COMMON CHALLENGES

The informants also agreed on a number of common challenges that confronted them in performing leadership roles in collaborative efforts. These included the challenges of visibility, communication, and risks.

Visibility

Informants noted that they often had a choice about whether they needed to be highly visible or quite invisible leaders as programs were planned. Their presence might not be needed, for example, if collaborators have had a successful history of working together and the program was one in a series. In other cases, a "hands-on" approach might be required, for example, when a relationship became fragile.

Informants noted that high visibility was required when new and/or large programs were being planned. Representatives of the staff development organization noted that "We work closely and very carefully with new and large programs, because many new organizations are involved, and the developing relationships, as well as the program planning, have to be closely monitored." The visible tasks that can be performed in these instances include planning and chairing meetings, following up on assignments, and keeping collaborators informed. Depending upon the situation, the leader may complete all of these tasks alone or with the assistance of staff. Of great importance in these situations are the direction, emphasis on task, and attention to the program's vision that the leader ensures. In this way individuals choose to perform the leadership roles of champion and strategy maker to ensure that the collaboration progresses effectively and that the program comes to fruition. As another example, the professional association director mentioned his role in a new program with European colleagues who were not familiar with the American association and were skeptical of its competence. "In that situation, I was involved from start to finish to prove my colleagues were wrong," he related. "And they were. The program was a very successful one."

The informants reported that they chose to be invisible for a variety of reasons. They admitted, for instance, that at times they lacked time to play visible leadership roles. In other cases they believed that it would be inappropriate to perform leadership roles, since others were better suited to do so because of experience or position. In still other instances they chose to be invisible to avoid the undue influence they might have on the process by virtue of their positions in their own organizations. They noted, for example, that if they were senior persons in a collaborative relationship, others might defer to their opinions. Without their presence a group of near equals could work more effectively together.

At times informants also chose to be invisible so that other members of their staff could gain experience in leading collaborative efforts. The professional association director and the park district manager agreed that stepping back to let staff take responsibility was sometimes more important than their direct involvement. In these circumstances, informants generally stayed away from meetings so that staff members could act without being influenced by or having to defer to their superiors. Even in these situations, informants remained engaged with the process by staying informed of progress, advising their staff members, doing work behind the scenes, and playing the role of a quiet, but valuable, program champion.

Informants also noted that they could choose to be visible at different stages in a collaborative relationship's development. They could, for example, play a very visible role at the start and become less active and visible once parameters were established and they were convinced that the group could function effectively. However, even in these cases, they retained the option of reentering the process and taking up a leadership role if they believed that their presence was needed.

The amount of visibility in leadership role performance

was therefore an issue with which informants grappled in each instance of collaboration. They made judgments about the level of required visibility based upon the unique circumstances of each collaborative situation they encountered.

Communication

Continuous written and oral communication was viewed by informants as a central ingredient in successful collaboration. They had to ensure that collaborators, leaders of partner organizations, other stakeholders, and potential program participants were constantly kept informed of the group's deliberations, progress, and successes. The importance of communication was evident in a number of comments offered by informants. The representatives of the staff development organization emphasized communication continually during the interview, noting on one occasion that "You can never over-communicate or over-inform in collaboration." The director of the professional association suggested that toner and paper are inexpensive when compared to the costs of not keeping collaborators and stakeholders informed. The director of the distance education consortium noted that communication had to go on regardless of the number of barriers that existed to reaching the people who needed the information. Maintaining this level of communication was therefore a challenge in the performance of all three major leadership roles, a challenge that all informants constantly stressed in their comments.

Risks

A final set of challenges centered on the amount of risk a leader could take in each situation. One risk was participating as an individual or as the representative of an organization in programs whose value was not readily apparent. Another risk was to be so visible and supportive of a program that the leader's reputation and image were tightly linked to the program and its success. How far to commit to leadership roles in these situations was a concern expressed by all informants.

Candor was a third risk. How truthful can leaders be when expressing their opinions? Will others correctly understand the points being made? Will they be able to benefit from criticism or will they take it personally? The association director made a special point of this when describing how he worked carefully with scientists from other parts of the world so as not to alienate them by being too candid.

Another risk had to do with the politics involved in planning programs. All of the informants mentioned that politics can and do play a significant role in collaboration, but the interests, conflict, and power associated with the political aspects of collaboration manifest themselves in different ways in various settings and planning situations. The professional association director mentioned how much he and his staff had to interact with government officials when they were planning programs to be held overseas. He added that he was the only one who could initially negotiate in some of these situations. He also noted how he worked carefully around an important opponent of a program in order to avoid alienating this individual and the organization he represented. By avoiding direct confrontation with this person, the collaborative effort progressed, the program was successfully offered and, as a result, the opponent became a supporter of both the program and the collaborative effort. Failure to deal with this political problem with finesse could have led to either a dissolution of the effort or the creation of an enemy.

The park district manager pointed out how politics affected the composition of planning committees, making it necessary to include some individuals who were not first choices and to exclude others who would have been preferred members. The informant from the consulting firm saw political issues as negative forces in her efforts to plan and offer an educational program. In this case, government agency personnel opposed her firm's conducting the program and set up barriers to progress. In addition, she faced resistance from outside groups that did not want the program to succeed. These groups lobbied against the program with the agency, thereby creating a political environment that complicated and compromised the collaborative effort. Power was a central issue in all of this wrangling—getting and holding it was the central agenda. The program became of secondary importance in spite of the value expected from it.

The staff development organization was faced with the challenge of building a niche as a valued organization and valued partner in the community. The organization also was confronted with a number of political issues, but acted to reduce their potential negative impact by concentrating efforts on relationship building and being seen as a neutral convener of parties with varied interests. As informants from this organization noted, "We also became the brokers and conveners that brought different groups together, and this too was to our advantage. Our neutral position made it easy for us to convene meetings and make initial arrangements that other collaborators could not."

Another risk identified by informants was being too conciliatory and too willing to compromise. Deciding if and when to compromise may be one of the hardest parts of collaboration, requiring adroit activity before, during, and after meetings. A balance has to be struck, the professional association director pointed out, between accommodating for the general good and allowing a group to make unsound decisions. "It is where I will point out what we have learned from experience about what will work," he said. "This involves a tremendous amount of tact, especially when dealing with colleagues from other parts of the world."

EFFECTIVE LEADERSHIP IN A COLLABORATIVE ENVIRONMENT

Several characteristics of effective leadership in collaboration became apparent as we reflected on informants' experiences with this type of programming. First and possibly foremost, these individuals were determined to see that a program idea became a reality. They knew that the program would be a sound one for their organization, other collaborators, and program participants.

Their ability and willingness to take risks also were evident. The risks were calculated and leveraged ones. Experience had taught them that a particular course of action had reasonably high potential for success. They made judgments about risk taking on the basis of their knowledge of those with whom they would have to work, the success rates for similar programs, and knowledge of the program's potential audience.

They evidenced a great deal of political savvy, especially about the issues that would likely attract conflict, and were sensitive to the potential sources of that conflict. They were willing to spend a reasonable amount of time dealing with the potential causes of those problems. When they took a step back from the actual planning, they could gauge progress, anticipate problems, and quietly repair strains in working relationships.

They firmly believed in the importance of communication. In all the leadership roles they performed, they worked to ensure that communication was continuous with all collaborators and other stakeholders.

All had a sense of what was feasible. They did not enter into collaborative arrangements that were so complicated and politically risky that success was unlikely. They worked incrementally and patiently, starting with smaller programs that had high potential for success. Program expansion could come once a program had an established niche and reputation.

The informants resisted complex formal relationships, believing that informal ones had a base in personal friendships and professional respect. Obviously some agreements had to be put in writing, but very detailed ones tended to limit action, rather than promote it.

The informants also shared a conviction about the importance of developing partnerships and having a vision for a program. Vision as described by informants had several common characteristics and served a set of common functions. Although developing and having a vision contributed to the work and relationships involved in collaboration, vision also played an important role for leaders as well. It is to their insights about vision that we now turn.

THE NECESSITY AND ROLE OF VISION

All of the informants were in agreement that a vision was central to the success of collaborative programs. They differed, however, in how detailed and explicit they believed that vision should be as collaborative work begins. Nonetheless, certain common characteristics of a vision did emerge from our interviews with them:

- The vision clearly communicated the outcomes of collaboration, especially the outcome of an excellent program.
- The vision also focused on the outcome of long-term working relationships with partners in future collaborative efforts.
- The vision captured the idea of program feasibility—the vision was compelling enough to draw participants to it, but was realistic enough that all knew that they could reach it without undue cost.
- The vision, to the extent possible, incorporated the varied interests represented by participating organizations.

In all cases, the vision drove leaders forward. It created the motivation to take the time to put the right group of cosponsors together. The informants talked about mental images of success that contributed to their planning and made the effort worthwhile. They were helped by past experiences which enabled them to sketch in words or pictures what the completion process would be like, how much work would be entailed, and what true collaboration meant. Especially as planning began, the creation of that mental picture was essential. From the vision flowed specific objectives, anticipated outcomes and the many details needed to make the educational program a memorable one.

Certainly, there would be disagreements about the vision as it was being shaped; that tension was discussed in Chapter 1 and its value described. And the disagreements might continue throughout the planning process. But the general shape of that vision would form a target that the planners were determined to reach. Those performing leadership roles and others involved in planning could continually return to the vision when planning strayed from the program's goals and desired outcomes.

The vision served another function. Informants spoke of the positive feeling that participants would have about the program. The vision contained a hopeful sense of the satisfaction that learners would gain from participation. Looking for ways to achieve this level of participant satisfaction became an unspoken program goal and led to inclusion of "participant-friendly" details that made the program all the better.

Based on the leader's experience, planners could be reminded of just how close they were getting to the desired vision. In addition, a mental picture of the program could be better created in written promotional materials. Persons promoting the program could demonstrate through their words the value of participation.

Finally, the vision was a useful post-program tool. After the program's conclusion, planners could measure the program against the vision for it, thereby using the vision as one of many tools for program evaluation. Planners could also assess what contributions the vision, and the processes through which it was sculpted, made to the collaborative effort itself. The results of these assessments could then be used to provide insights about the type of vision required for such programming, and about the processes that could be employed to develop a vision in future collaborative efforts.

CONCLUSION

Clearly, leadership and vision are critical elements in collaborative relationships and programming. Leadership is required to convene stakeholders, to champion the program, and to develop strategies that enhance the growth of the collaborative relationship in ways that permit work to get accomplished. A compelling and vital vision draws support to the program and serves as part of the "glue" that holds collaborators together as the program is planned and offered. In fact, these components are so critical to success in collaboration that they will be treated again in remaining chapters, but from different perspectives. Vision is addressed in the next chapter from the perspective of the tension involved in developing a vision. It is to the consideration of this tension, as well as other tensions and changes experienced in collaboration, that we now turn.

CHAPTER 4

Tensions and Transformations in Relationship Building and Maintenance

Five major process themes were identified from the data provided by informants. Each highlights the forces and transformations that informants experienced in the collaborative efforts in which they had been involved. The themes also underscore the dynamic nature of collaboration across and within its development stages. For this reason, they draw our attention again to many of the dynamic processes and tensions introduced in Chapter 1. But in doing so they also bring these processes and tensions to life, add detail, and present them as they are dealt with by real people in real situations. The themes capture five major tensions with which people must deal in collaboration. These are tensions between

- developing a vision and having a vision that attracts collaborators and guides action,
- informal and formal means of governance,
- accomplishing work and building and sustaining relationships,
- risk taking and risk avoidance, and
- stability and transformation.

These five themes are the focus of this chapter.

DEVELOPING A VISION VERSUS HAVING A VISION

As noted in Chapter 3, a shared vision is needed to hold a team of collaborators together and provide direction. A compelling and attractive vision also serves several other purposes, including attracting potential collaborators, motivating them, and serving as an important post-program tool for evaluation. Although having a vision was important to informants, equally important was the process by which it was developed. As informants from the staff development organization noted, "The process reveals individual viewpoints and personalities, serves as a means to establish open communications, trust, and respect." In short, while vision is a product to be created, developing the vision also serves as an initial and ongoing process to build and maintain relationships throughout the collaboration. Therefore, this tension highlights an important dynamic in collaboration.

This tension required informants to view vision not as a static element in collaboration, but as an evolving one. In dealing with this understanding of vision and the tensions surrounding it, informants developed several principles of practice to guide their management of this tension. For example, the informants from the staff development organization believed strongly that vision should be tied to the initial understanding of the real educational needs of the people who were to be served, and must be a priority of both the partner organizations and their representatives. While recognizing this principle, the director of the professional association also drew attention to the fact that organizations and their representatives enter collaboration with organizational and individual interests, but not necessarily a vision. Therefore, in order to gain commitment to the undertaking and the program it produces, it is essential that these varied interests be translated into a vision that incorporates elements of the different interests represented. Informants also noted that the process often involves compromise on the part of collaborators, always demands that they come to understand and appreciate their different interests, and always compels learning together about what the collaboration is supposed to be doing and why.

In developing the vision the professional association director suggested that it is very helpful for the convener to have a vision statement prepared to present to collaborators orally, if not in writing, when they first convene. This initial version must, however, be viewed as a springboard for working and learning together, and as a statement that will be changed. As the vision is changed during the emergence and later stages of development, it is also important for all participants to "let go" of earlier versions. These earlier versions can be remembered as part of the collaboration's history and as milestones in its development. But they must not remain operative as guides to future direction, action, or as a basis for holding collaborators together.

Informants also recognized that the vision may change only slightly throughout the effort, change dramatically, or even be rejected at any developmental stage, depending upon a variety of internal and external factors. Change of any magnitude may have one of two effects. It may strengthen the vision and in turn the relationship. Or, change may impact the vision adversely, creating stress in the relationship. Therefore, informants viewed vision development and change as an important process to be monitored and managed with care. Informants also clearly distinguished between vision and goals and objectives. The director of the distance education consortium noted, for example, that when the vision came into question in later stages of collaboration, he attempted first to change goals and objectives, leaving change of vision as a strategy of last resort, given its potential impact on the relationship. The point of their insights is simply this: The extent to which a vision exists and the extent to which it is changed will have much to do with the work of collaborators and the health of their relationship throughout the entire process. Considering vision only a product is insufficient, as is viewing its development as only one of the processes of collaboration. Both definitions and understanding of them are essential in initiating, developing, and maintaining a successful collaborative effort.

FORMAL VERSUS INFORMAL GOVERNANCE

As noted in Chapter 1, a balance of informal and formal governance is required for a collaboration to be healthy and work well. Informants had somewhat different perspectives on how this balance was to be achieved.

The park district manager, the professional association director, and the director of the local government education program preferred informal governance structures unless sharing of costs, losses, and profits were involved. Even when formal written agreements were called for, they preferred that agreements be as simple and straightforward as possible, leaving problems, directions, roles, responsibilities, and relationships to be worked out by organizational representatives. The professional association director actually viewed formal written agreements as a hindrance to collaboration. In his opinion, the negotiations associated with them took valuable time and energy away from program development. He also believed that informal processes worked best because they made collaborative work more personally enjoyable and potentially more efficient. Informal processes allow collaborators who have a history of collaborative relationships to get moving faster—the "wheel does not have to be reinvented," as would be the case if agreements had to be formalized before program planning proceeded.

Although neither of these informants preferred written agreements, this did not mean that they were without formal, albeit unwritten, agreements that guided the collaborative effort. The professional association chose whenever possible to cover all costs, take all financial risks, and handle all logistical details of programming. As a result, agreement about roles and responsibilities was prescribed for collaborators up front: The professional association was responsible for program finances, logistics, and facilitating program design; other collaborators were responsible for participating in shaping the vision for the program, deciding content, collaborating in designing the program, and identifying, selecting, and obtaining instructors and speakers. The park district's programs were generally less complex than the professional association's, primarily involving only a few cosponsors, and sharing of facilities and other nonmonetary resources. As a consequence, its agreements were more informal and the need for written agreements was reserved for situations in which sharing of finances was involved or the complexity of programs grew to proportions where formal written agreements were required to stipulate different organizations' roles and responsibilities.

In contrast, the staff development organization informants indicated that they always preferred some form of written agreement. In their opinion, without a written set of expectations, assumptions about different collaborators' roles and responsibilities could frequently go awry. Yet, these written agreements were not highly complex. Rather, they were crisp and succinct statements of collaborators' expectations of each other. This organization's preference for written agreement was in part a function of the scope of its collaborative efforts and the complexity of the programs to which collaboration contributed. Its projects tended to last several years, involve up to 10 or more organizations, and focus on systemic change programs rather than isolated educational offerings. Although this organization's representatives preferred to have formal written expectations, they still noted that a balance between formal and informal governance was essential to collaboration: "The formal and informal [agreements] work in tandem—if you have a formal agreement with no informal, norms based, psychological and social contract that goes beyond the formal, the partnership is not effective."

Other informants tended to collaborate most frequently within the context of formal written agreements. The distance education consortium functioned within the context of a legislative statute that mandated collaboration. The consulting firm had a formal written contract with the government agency. The local government education program had formal contracts with a number of sponsoring foundations. The universities jointly offering the graduate degree program had a formal letter of agreement and were governed by their institution's boards as well as by policies and program approval provided by the state's coordinating board for higher education.

Yet all four organizations found ways to develop informal governance mechanisms within these very formal contexts, thereby striking the necessary balance between these two forces. The distance education consortium used informal approaches to establish procedures for carrying out the business of the collaborative effort. A trusting, norm-based relationship among individuals guided the consulting firm and government agency in their early work together. The formal contract served as a statement of intent, while the vision, responsibilities, and other details of the effort were allowed to evolve and change and even vary from the letter of the contract as the relationship developed. The relationship became process governed as opposed to rule governed within the confines of a formal contract.

Formal agreements were necessary when the local government education program contracted with specific institutions to conduct programs. However, for over the nearly 20 years of this program's operation, informal letters of understanding had been sufficient when working with state agencies and local government associations. The universities relied upon trusting, norm-based relationships in carrying out their respective duties in planning and offering the collaborative graduate program. At one point, a university threatened not to fulfill a commitment it had made. The leader of this project relied on the established norms of the relationship rather than a formal written agreement or position of authority to remind the representative of his university's moral obligation, and thereby secured the resources it had committed. These examples demonstrate the dynamic, social, and moral dimensions of informal psychological and social contracts that act in powerful ways to govern collaborative work. They also demonstrate that such informal governance structures have the potential for existing alongside and within the context of highly formalized agreements.

This review of the way balance was struck in these different collaborative efforts highlights four major points. First, the balance required between formal and informal governance mechanisms will differ according to a variety of situational factors, including characteristics of partner organizations, the complexity of programs, the anticipated length of the effort, the number of partner organizations involved, and the history of previous working relationships. Second, formal written agreements appear to be most necessary when finances are involved, when working for the first time with a new organization, when the collaboration exists within a structured format (like a government contract) and when collaboration lasts a long time and change in personnel is anticipated. Third, if written agreements are required they should be kept as simple and straightforward as possible. Fourth, balance between formal and informal governance mechanisms is essential. Managing this balance is a major challenge in collaboration.

ACCOMPLISHING WORK VERSUS BUILDING AND SUSTAINING RELATIONSHIPS

The previous two sections, on vision versus developing the vision and on the formal/informal tensions in governance, foreshadow a related tension—between getting work done and building and maintaining relationships. This is a tension because attending to program-related work at the expense of relationship development is problematic. But so too is a focus on relationship building at the expense of getting the work done and the program offered. Again, this is a tension between related elements, since working effectively depends on strong relationships, and accomplishments contribute to the development of strong relationships.

Although each of our informants identified this tension, each also recommended that relationship development should be an initial priority. As representatives of the staff development organization noted, developing the norms of how a group is to work together is as important as developing a common vision. Members of the collaborative effort must therefore address this question early in the process: "How do we want to be treated as part of this partnership?" The representatives of the staff development organization strongly suggested that norms and consequences of violating them must be discussed and established early in the process. As part of establishing these norms, it was also important that members of the partnership make their assumptions explicit for the rest of the group. Without this candid sharing of assumptions, the probability that trust will be stretched thin or sabotaged is increased tremendously. These same representatives gave an example of how they acted to establish one norm in a recent collaborative effort. In meetings of partners, they suggested and continually reinforced the need for partners to always ask: "How am I involving my partner?" This norm required partners to continually take others into account as they worked on tasks associated with the vision and goals of the partnership. Acting on this norm facilitated communication, built trust, and enabled the partnership to develop through mutual adjustment among members.

Building the relationship does not need to be accomplished, however, at the total exclusion of getting work done. Frequently, relationship building was addressed by several informants through certain work tasks, such as establishing an early version of the vision. The staff development organization informants also shared another way they built relationships through work. When collaborative partner organizations were provided grant funding to hire additional staff members, they made the hiring of these additional staff members "transparent." They shared the criteria for search and selection, sought input from other partners, and even let other partners participate in decision making about hiring. This helped ensure that new staff members would be able to work together as a team within the partnership structure. It also built communication and trust, thereby strengthening the relationship.

Two other themes pervaded informants' comments about the relationship between getting work done and building relationships. These themes were the importance of membership and small successes.

Membership

The membership of a collaborative effort impacts both the strength of the relationship and the collaborative effort's effectiveness in getting work done. The informants provided several insights about how to obtain adequate membership and the correct mix of members.

Number

Katzenbach and Smith (1993), as well as informants, suggested that smaller groups (between 5 and 25 members) function better than larger ones because their sense of community is heightened and members can more easily work through their differences and hold themselves mutually accountable for results. Informants maintained relatively small groups, especially for decision-making purposes. However, they also devised ways to increase involvement of representatives from participating organizations in order to gain ownership in the program from as many constituents as possible and to capitalize on the insights and work that others could contribute to program development and delivery. The professional association director involved as many people in collaboration as he could, but he did so by defining several different ways that people could contribute. A small group was responsible for direction and vision setting, decision making, and establishing policy. Larger groups of people from participating organizations were invited to contribute their insights about program content, presenters, and other programmatic issues.

The graduate department hosting the cohort program used a similar strategy. A council of college deans oversaw major policy and financial decisions about the program. A coordinating committee of about 10 people was responsible for curriculum development, policy, and procedures for the program. A much larger group of faculty members (more than 40 people) participated in developing broad outlines for courses. This broader involvement contributed to building ownership of the program among a large group of faculty members from partner universities. Small teams of faculty members were used to finalize the curriculum for each course and to deliver instruction. Therefore, when developing a sense of community, dealing with differences, and building trusting relationships were essential, smaller groups were used. Larger groups of representatives were employed for other purposes.

Member Characteristics and Mix

Informants had several suggestions about the characteristics one should look for in representatives from participating organizations. The director of the professional association recommended that representatives be highly successful, powerful, and highly competent people who can make decisions for their organizations. The park district manager had similar advice and also commented on the need to avoid representatives who could not make decisions for their organizations, since the presence of such individuals tended to create stress in the effort. In short, representatives are needed who bring a variety of competencies to the effort, who are powerful enough to build support for the program within their organizations, and who can make decisions and commitments without checking with others.

Informants from the staff development organization added two additional recommendations. First, they suggested that representatives who tend to enjoy synthesis contribute more to collaboration than those who do not. Given the need to develop a shared vision, merge complementary and perhaps competing interests through processes of mutual adjustment, and develop new ways of thinking and programming, these characteristics indeed appear to be ideal for collaboration. Second, they recommended that representatives be individuals who are not adversely affected by any negative history that organizations might have in working together. Most informants mentioned that for certain programs it was important to convene organizations which may have had poor experiences with each other. However, by involving representatives who have not been negatively affected by this history, much of the potential for the partnership to be affected by this negative organizational "baggage" can be avoided.

Informants also highlighted the importance of conveners not overlooking the importance of including critics and "naysayers" in the mix of representatives. Informants distinguished between these types of individuals and those who were truly enemies. As noted in Chapter 3, critics are important because they raise valuable questions, forcing other representatives to question their assumptions, think about new ways of doing things, and develop a sound and defensible rationale for their actions. Naysayers are individuals who believe that the collaborative program will never work. The professional association director recounted an experience in which the representative of a major organization (one that could not be left out of the partnership) continued to believe through planning that the program would never be offered successfully. Members of the collaboration took great care not to alienate this naysayer, by not confronting him and thereby making him an enemy. Instead they worked around him and continued to make progress in program planning and implementation. The program turned out to be very successful. As a result, the naysayer became a supporter of the program and the collaboration that led to it. Thus, by involving this person and dealing with him carefully, the professional association was able to gain a valuable ally for future efforts. The local government education program staff used the same approach and built a strong network of supporters who initially had to be convinced to cooperate. Still other persons may participate in a collaborative effort, not so much to contribute to it, but to protect their organizations' interests (Smutz & Toombs, 1985). Therefore, by recognizing the different reasons organizations and their representatives participate and taking care not to alienate them, it is possible (although not ensured) that their support may also be earned through program success.

Finally, informants strongly recommended that representatives possess different and complementary sets of core competencies. These should not be limited to task or work competencies. They should also include process competencies, or those which contribute to developing and maintaining the relationship. For example, the director of the local government advisory program noted the importance of having on collaborative planning committees both "openers," people who can brainstorm ideas and "closers," individuals who help the group come to decision. Other process competencies include the ability to be open to new ideas and, through a variety of group process skills, to facilitate the ongoing development of the relationship among members.

Small Successes

All informants spoke of the importance of small successes throughout all developmental stages. These successes mark important milestones in the work of the group, but they also help sustain the relationship by building motivation, increasing enthusiasm, and reinforcing the incentives for organizations to invest in the arrangement. Small successes come in multiple forms. Informants identified the following examples—agreeing on vision, goals, and objectives, building and maintaining the relationship itself, inspiring enthusiasm among collaborators, meeting deadlines, getting outstanding speakers, keeping people posted through adequate communication, sharing progress, since progress itself is a success, and having good, productive meetings.

The kinds of success required are those in which all participating organizations can share. As the park manager noted, "everyone must come out a winner." However, for successes to be shared, responsibilities must first be divided among partners so all have a significant stake in them. Additionally, these responsibilities must be "doable"—discrete enough for partners to accomplish so they can demonstrate and share success with others. Several informants also reminded us that participants in collaborative ventures are sometimes volunteers, with limited time and resources. Therefore, strategies must be used to get work done while not overwhelming those who perform it. Informants suggested two major strategies for accomplishing this. First, tasks should be narrowly rather than broadly defined, and those with more time and resources (for example, paid staff of a major participating organization) should coordinate and monitor the work being done. Second certain tasks, like the detail work of programming, should be delegated to a partner organization's staff.

Representatives of the staff development organization added an important corollary principle to small successes—mutual accountability, an essential characteristic of high performing teams (Katzenbach & Smith, 1993). To create mutual accountability, several informants recommended that milestones and deadlines be developed and communicated in writing to all. They also noted the importance of jointly establishing measures of success for these milestones. Having these measures increases the likelihood that partners will recognize when they have successfully achieved a milestone.

Informants noted, however, that small successes are insufficient unless they are also celebrated and communicated. Celebration of success serves an important symbolic function in sustaining the relationship. Through celebration ceremonies, the meanings of collaboration and of the vision are communicated and reinforced. By communicating successes, constituencies, especially leaders in partner organizations, are kept informed of progress and the results of their investment in the effort.

Although maintaining appropriate balance between work and relationships, formal and informal governance structures, and developing and having a vision lead to both small and large successes, maintaining this balance is also accompanied by maintaining an appropriate balance between taking and avoiding risks, especially risks to the relationship.

RISK TAKING VERSUS RISK AVOIDANCE

Collaborative efforts face many risks. These include financial risks, credibility risks, and political risks. But, there are also relationship risks, risks that come in the form of threats to fair dealing, which includes issues of equity, trust, and reciprocity. Ring and Van de Ven (1994) have noted that the greatest risks faced in collaborative efforts are the risks to fair dealing and trust. Support is given to this observation by our informants who mentioned this type of risk far more frequently than those of economy, politics, or image. As informants from the staff development organization noted, every collaborative effort has its "psychological [risks] of having to trust others and having to think about things differently." In addition, we found that these risks manifested themselves in different ways and occurred in all three developmental stages of collaboration.

Risks to equity come in the form of failure of one or more partner organizations to fulfill its obligations. The staff development organization described its experiences with collaborative efforts in which a partner organization did not follow through on responsibilities, leaving the rest of the group holding the bag. The professional association director mentioned that he has had numerous experiences with organizational representatives not carrying their fair load on the collaborative team. The park district manager shared an instance in which he learned just before program implementation that the funds expected from one partner organization would not be forthcoming. Each of these events occurred at various times during the evolution and implementation stages of development. As defined in Chapter 1, equity is the perception that the benefits of participating in a collaborative effort are proportional to the organization's investment. When either a partner organization or its representative does not fulfill its share of responsibilities, the investments of other organizations increase, drawing into question whether the collaboration remains an equitable one.

Threats to reciprocity, or the diffuse and generalized obligation one person or organization has to another person or organization, were found to occur in both the emergence and evolution stages. The professional association director recounted an experience in which he worked for over a year with a trade association to gain agreement on a vision for a program. The trade association was unbending, sensing that the program as envisioned by the partner organizations was a threat to its interests. As a result, the trade association was eventually dropped from the partnership, creating a threat to future collaboration between the two organizations. The professional association director also mentioned experiences in which, due to a change in vision, partner organizations lost interest in collaborating and removed themselves from the effort. Their withdrawal created bad feelings and damaged any sense of reciprocity that existed or that could have been cultivated. The park district manager shared an experience with a governmental agency's failure to fully share its agenda when initiating a seemingly collaborative effort. Once the collaboration began it became apparent that the agency wanted only to fulfill its own interests and dominate the joint effort. Its action not only damaged the trust the park district manager had in the other organization and its representatives, but it also interfered with his obligation to work with the agency in the future. In all these instances, the obligation to work with another organization or person was damaged, decreasing the potential for the organizations to collaborate in the future.

Threats to trust also were manifested in many ways. The actions of the governmental agency noted above undermined the level of trust the park district manager could put in this organization and its representatives. The informants from the staff development organization gave examples of collaborators using another organization's proprietary information in unethical ways, or using organizational weaknesses identified during collaboration to gain a competitive edge over partner organizations in other venues. The director of the local government education program pointed out that some organizations would come to one or two planning meetings, and then proceed on their own to develop programs similar to the ones being planned by the collaborative group. In this instance, collaboration created an opportunity for these organizations to sit with the competition disguised as potential partners only to use the information and ideas discussed to compete directly with the programs being planned collaboratively. In all three cases, the social and psychological contracts between the organizations were violated, leaving them feeling hurt, alienated, and at much risk.

Threats to fair dealing create stress for a relationship by changing interpersonal dynamics. In order to anticipate and deal with these stresses, it is critically important for the relationship to be monitored, with particular attention to the changes it is experiencing.

STABILITY VERSUS TRANSFORMATION

Transformation or change in a collaborative effort can occur at any stage in its development. Some transformations may have a positive impact on the effort, acting to strengthen it in important ways and, at times, even to reduce stress that has developed in a relationship. Other transformations, while positive, are nonetheless sources of stress to which the partnership must adapt if it is to capitalize on the positive potential of these changes. Still other transformations occur as a result of problems within the collaborative relationship itself. If these problems are not identified and addressed the collaboration will be severely weakened. Examples of these three types of transformation are provided in the following paragraphs.

Positive Transformations

Some changes strengthen collaborative relationships. Sometimes they are the milestones toward which collaborators are working. For example, receipt of state funding to support the collaborative graduate program solidified already strong relationships, provided credence to the program's vision, and reinforced the work of participating universities and their representatives. It also increased participants' motivation and commitment to work together. Through advice from different planning groups, the local government education program was able to turn state programs into regional and national ones. This transformation broadened both the program's reach and image, and in doing so also strengthened the relationship among partner organizations. Other positive transformations occur more by chance. A change in leadership in a participating organization may introduce a person more committed to the effort than the previous leader, thereby strengthening the organization's commitment to the program and thus the strength of the relationship.

Other positive transformations occur as a result of work

done by collaborators or by members who play leadership roles. In addition to strengthening the relationship, they relieve existing stresses. According to the director of the distance education consortium, obtaining funding to hire staff to oversee its operations solved a problem by removing a stressful element from the collaborative effort. Having a staff person handle day-to-day details allowed representatives to focus less on operational issues and more on policy and program development and on building support for the collaborative effort at their own institutions. The director of the professional association reported instances in which he or others in leadership roles were able to replace an unenthusiastic organizational representative with one more committed to and enthusiastic about the program. This resulted in both solving a problem and improving the relationship and the program.

These transformations contribute to the collaborative effort because they contribute to positive assessments of equity and efficiency. They permit proper balances between risk taking and risk avoidance, between formality and informality, and between work and relationships to be maintained and even strengthened. But not all positive changes lead naturally to these results. Some introduce stresses that must be addressed.

Positive, but Challenging Transformations

The park district manager described an educational program that grew in size geometrically from one year to the next: "We did not anticipate the level of community interest; our predictions of how many would participate were far too low." Although a very positive development from a programmatic point of view, the size of the program quickly outstripped the capacity of collaborating organizations to cope with it in adequate fashion, creating a variety of stresses. First, it took attention away from other park district programs, putting pressure on already busy staff and volunteers. Second, to cope with the program's growth, planning time was taken from other programs as needed. This meant that promotional materials for other programs came out late, putting their enrollments at risk. In addition, more time had to be put into changing the makeup of the collaborative arrangement itself. More cosponsors had to be recruited, the size of the planning committee had to be enlarged, and a larger budget planned and the monies for it found.

Fortunately, this partnership was able to adapt to the rapid growth of its program. Growth did not change the vision that had held the group together and guided its efforts, and relationships and commitments to the program were sufficiently strong to permit adjustments without putting either at serious risk. To maintain equity and efficiency in the effort, the group was willing to grow larger by inviting other organizations to participate. The success of the program and its compelling vision assisted in attracting additional organizations to the effort. Still, this change required additional work of the program's champions, compelled individuals to play the convener role again in order to attract more organizations, and exacted a cost to the park district and other collaborating organizations in putting their other programs at risk as they took time to address the challenges posed by this program's growth. In short, the resiliency of the collaboration, developed over time through commitment to each other and the program, and the willingness of collaborators to revisit roles they had played earlier, allowed this challenging, but positive, transformation to be addressed in a way that benefitted all participating organizations and the community.

Negative Transformations

Although many of the transformations experienced by collaborative endeavors are positive, others can be quite negative. The representative of the consulting firm provided a very instructive example. She experienced tremendous success in earlier collaborative efforts with the governmental agency and the professional associations affiliated with it. Planning went smoothly, relationships and trust with the agency's leadership and with her primary contacts grew increasingly strong. By all reports, not only were participating organizations satisfied with the relationship, but individuals also were gaining much personal satisfaction from it. Visions for programs had been established with full participation of partners. The formal contract served not as a limit to what could be done, but as a guide or statement of parameters and intents within which deviations could be made as relationships developed and visions and tasks were fine tuned. Programs were successfully offered, with many accolades and credits shared among all participating organizations. Things went so well that an additional collaborative arrangement, again within the context of a formal contract, began. In this case, previous success clearly contributed to additional collaboration.

Things began to change, however, soon after the latest collaborative effort began. First, the consultants' primary contacts in the agency were assigned other duties and were no longer able to participate in the collaboration. Then the political environment of the agency changed dramatically. Its current level of funding was no longer secure, creating not only general problems for the agency but also affecting the work of agency leaders who had been supportive of past programs. The agency became increasingly less communicative and responsive. Information was no longer shared as freely or as frequently as in the past. Identification of individuals to replace the agency's previous contact persons took months instead of days or weeks. When new contacts were identified, relationships did not blossom as in the past. The new contacts did not take on the mantle of program champions. Agreement on a vision for the program was not forthcoming and trust was at an all time low. The consultant did not trust others in the collaborative relationship, and she began to wonder whether other individuals trusted her. All discussions were put in writing, and roles and responsibilities were formalized rather than established informally. The contract became the "letter of the law," rather than a guide to action. The relationship became a very fragile one. But because it had been initiated within the context of a contract, it could not be ended.

This example points out several dimensions of negative

transformations. Change in personnel creates stress for a collaborative arrangement. This change can be even more stressful if the individual lost has played a major leadership role. In this case, the balance between formal and informal governance was not maintained. Formality ruled, limiting the ability of the collaboration to govern itself through informal, processual means. Getting the job done and fulfilling the contract began to take precedence over building and maintaining relationships. The psychological contract that had guided the collaborative relationship up until recently was broken. Trust was gone and risks were being averted rather than taken. The personal satisfaction that comes from working collaboratively with others was replaced with the dissatisfaction of having to work in a stressful, inefficient environment where relationships were poor. Unfortunately, there was no way to dissolve the relationship. Reciprocity was no longer present, and the probability of the same organizations collaborating again was reduced tremendously.

This, perhaps, is an extreme example of a relationship that became very fragile. But even under the best of circumstances problems arise within a partnership that can rapidly lead to fragility and dissolution. Some of these developments are simply out of the control of the partners. A sudden loss of funding to support programming is one example. In this instance, partners must either adapt to these transformations (for example, by quickly finding other sources of financial support) or face the specter of revising its vision or ending the effort prematurely. Other negative transformations can be addressed by collaborators. However, addressing them requires recognition of their attendant danger signals.

Danger Signals

Bergquist, Betwee, and Meuel (1995) have noted that a decline in the quantity and quality of direct communication among collaborators is a central symptom that negative transformations are taking place. And, as the consultant's example illustrates, a decline in communication is a signal that a collaborative effort is in trouble. But informants also shared other danger signals that appeared at all stages in the development of their collaborative efforts.

These danger signals can be classified into 11 broad categories which are decrease in commitment, loss of financial resources, irreconcilable differences, changes in personnel, loss of vision, change in language, domination, imbalance in formality/informality, role and relationship diffusion, growth, and individuals' needs and satisfaction.

Decrease in Commitment

Decrease in commitment can manifest itself in various ways. Signs of a decrease in commitment include the following:

1. Meeting attendance declines.
2. Collaborators increasingly send substitutes to meetings instead of attending themselves.
3. Organizational representatives who attend meetings are unable to make decisions for their organizations.
4. Enthusiasm for the program diminishes and barriers to success are increasingly discussed.
5. Past collaborative efforts are discussed, sometimes with nostalgic reference to their success.
6. Individual representatives and their organizations fail to follow through with their responsibilities and become increasingly unresponsive to deadlines.
7. Organizations withdraw their support.

Loss of Financial Resources

Resources may be lost due to external, uncontrollable, circumstances, or because they are withdrawn by an individual organization. The park district manager learning that financial support would not be forthcoming from a partner organization is an example of the latter. However, loss of financial resources need not weaken a collaborative effort if partners anticipate that alternative sources of funding must be obtained. The local government education program was funded initially by foundation grants. Yet, partners knew that this funding would eventually end. They began to identify alternative sources of funding almost as soon as collaboration began. Recognizing this danger sign in advance led to maintenance of this collaborative effort for more than twenty years.

Irreconcilable Differences

Organizations may simply have irreconcilable differences in values, interests, objectives, and working philosophies. This was the case in the example of the trade association that, for over a year, was unwilling to compromise its interests to collaborate with the professional association. Although this example occurred in the emergence stage of development, irreconcilable differences may surface during other stages as well. The director of the professional association cited instances in which the vision for an effort changed over time. With this change, differences surfaced that were so incompatible that certain organizations chose to leave the collaboration.

Changes in Personnel

This theme was echoed throughout all informants' comments. They also emphasized the magnified impact that loss of leadership has for efforts. The park district manager recounted an experience when a program champion left a partnership. Following the champion's departure, meetings became social gatherings instead of working meetings, and the park district manager feared that the collaboration would end unless another organization was willing to take on the role of program champion.

Loss of Vision

Visions often change, but they can also simply be lost. This may occur because of changing environmental circumstances, sufficient change in personnel that the vision is no longer shared, or failure to continually revisit the vision to keep it vital and compelling. Loss of vision may be signaled by a decrease in the frequency of mentioning and discussing it. As vision loses its integrative and compelling force, members of the collaboration may be unwilling to confront this reality.

Change in Language

Although a decrease in the quantity and quality of communication is a sign of problems, so too is even a subtle change in the content of communication. The consulting firm representative noticed that as problems increased in her last collaborative effort, agency personnel began to talk about her previous contacts in less than glowing ways. To her, this signaled a change in the agency's commitment to the collaboration or at least to its opinion of their previous collaboration.

Domination

During a collaboration one or more partners may attempt to dominate decision making and direction setting. Such organizations attempt to control the agenda in order to meet their vested interests. The experience of the park district manager with a domineering government agency is illustrative of this danger sign.

Imbalance in Formality/Informality

Collaborative efforts may become either too informal or too formal. The example provided by the consulting firm's representative illustrates a case in which collaboration was out of balance in the direction of formality. Putting everything in writing and letting the contract be the absolute arbiter of what could be done slowed program planning and interfered with the natural development of psychological and social contracts. In contrast, as informants from the staff development organization noted, too much informality lets assumptions run awry. Partners incorrectly assume that other collaborators have responsibility for certain tasks. The work does not get done and trust and equity are threatened. Some level of formal governance, if only a simple list of agreements, helps maintain the balance needed between formal and informal governance. It allows the differentiation of roles and responsibilities to be understood by all, and thereby prevents assumptions that may be harmful to the relationship.

Role and Relationship Diffusion

If roles and relationships are not differentiated, the work of the collaborative effort is threatened. Too much informal governance does not create the necessary structure for work to be parceled out and integrated. As a result, program planning and implementation may proceed in an inefficient, haphazard way. Relationships may also become strained as a result of collaborators not understanding the roles and responsibilities of all involved. Again, balance between formal and informal governance is required.

Growth

If the collaborative project grows too large, a sense of community may be lost. Informants did not mention this as a danger sign, probably because they kept policy and decision-making bodies relatively small. By involving organizational representatives in multiple tasks, they were able to capitalize on a wide range of skills without compromising the partners' sense of community. Thus, growth can be managed by controlling the number of people involved in different kinds of activity. When relationships, effective teamwork, and a sense of community are essential to success, smaller groups work best.

Individuals' Needs and Satisfaction

Personal satisfaction plays a large part in making collaboration successful. It is fostered when personal needs are met and individuals feel that they are making contributions to something important. When people are not satisfied, they exhibit certain behaviors that signal that their needs require attention. Some of the danger signs that relate to this individual dimension of collaboration include the following:

1. Organizations and their representatives feel that they are being used by the collaboration instead of making a contribution to it.
2. People show signs of frustration and anger.
3. Friendship is replaced by courtesy.
4. Individuals feel they have been blindsided by others.
5. Individuals show signs of having difficulty dealing with the distant time horizons of collaborative ventures and the ambiguity frequently associated with them, especially during early stages of development.

The fact that these signals may be associated with an individual makes them no less important. They point out needs that are not being met within the context of collaboration. Some of these signals are also related to trust. Being blindsided and feeling used threaten the trust that these individuals put in other members of the group. This brings us again to the threat to fair dealing, one of the more serious dangers for collaboration. In this case, the threat compromises individual needs and satisfaction rather than those of the organizations they represent.

CONCLUSION

In this chapter we have highlighted many of the forces at work in collaboration and described the balance that must be achieved among them if the undertaking is to be successful. We have also illustrated the different types of transformations these endeavors experience throughout their developmental stages. Recognizing, understanding and being sensitive to these elements, are essential to wise use of collaboration in the planning and delivery of educational programs. But recognition, understanding, awareness, and sensitivity alone are insufficient. Adult and continuing education professionals also need ways to identify forces, transformations, and strategies for ensuring the proper balance between the competing forces of collaborative enterprises. These strategies include monitoring, building trust, communicating effectively, and dealing with differences.

CHAPTER 5

Strategies for Sustaining and Ending Collaborative Relationships

In the previous chapter our attention was focused on the many tensions that must be balanced in collaboration and on the changes that may affect partnerships in a variety of ways. In this chapter we turn our attention to a series of strategies that individuals can use to sustain collaborative relationships. We also address strategies for ending collaborative efforts if a decision is made that they are not worth salvaging.

Until recently the primary focus of literature on collaboration has addressed decision making about entering a collaborative arrangement. Much less has been written about sustaining and maintaining relationships, or ending them once the decision has been made to collaborate. As we have thought about the understanding garnered from the limited literature on relationship maintenance and reflected upon the experience and insights of our informants, we have concluded that strategies for relationship maintenance can be organized around six broad topics:

- Monitoring the collaborative relationship and its work
- Building trust and communicating
- Dealing with differences
- Resting and growing
- Developing effective teamwork
- Dealing with fragile relationships

Each of these topics will be considered in turn in this chapter.

MONITORING THE COLLABORATIVE RELATIONSHIP AND ITS WORK

As noted in the last chapter, transformations within and outside the collaborative relationship can affect it in a variety of ways. These transformations require constant monitoring and anticipation on the part of the collaborative team. Information gathered from monitoring activities and from anticipating potential problems allows generation of alternative plans, fine tuning and improvement of tasks and approaches, capitalization on positive developments, and addressing developments that create stress and/or weaken collaboration.

Our informants highlighted the value of monitoring in several ways. The professional association director noted that it " . . . forces you to take a step back and stand apart from what you are doing to evaluate it." The director of the local government education program cast monitoring within the context of anticipating problems. He noted that, "Thinking about worst case scenarios is valuable. Monitoring what you are doing and anticipating potential difficulties allow you to develop alternative plans, putting you in a better position to deal with the unexpected." In some collaborative efforts no monitoring goes on. In these instances, a successful educational program may result, but luck rather than planning will have produced the desired results. None of our informants relied on luck. Rather, they constantly watched, both formally and informally, all aspects of their collaborative efforts. All of the informants constantly scanned the internal and external environments to determine if steady progress was being made. If progress was not being made they also sought information to help them understand why this was the case.

Responsibility for Monitoring

In considering the strategy of monitoring, one must attend to three major issues: (a) Who should do the monitoring? (b) What should be monitored? and (c) What sources of information can be tapped? Clearly, persons who assume leadership roles must play a central part in monitoring, as in other aspects of the collaborative effort. The convener must be able to scan the external environment to identify program opportunities and pinpoint interested stakeholders who can be invited to join the collaborative effort. The strategy maker must have access to information to channel it, identify and allocate resources, and keep the work of the group on track. The product champion has to monitor progress in order to share successes and be an effective advocate for the program.

Although monitoring activities and anticipating problems are the responsibilities of those who assume leadership roles, both activities are performed far more effectively when the collaborative team performs them collectively. The different representatives of a collaborative relationship have more access to a variety of information channels, sources, and pieces of information than any one person can possibly possess. Additionally, each team member can provide different and valuable interpretations of the same information, providing insight about both subtle and dramatic changes in the project. The consulting firm representative recounted an experience in which a representative of a partner organization not only provided additional information about that partner, but also offered an insightful interpretation of information already available. These contributions helped the consultant deal with stress in that particular relationship. Therefore, monitoring should be the joint responsibility of both leaders and other members of the team. Introducing and assigning this responsibility to all partners early in the process appears to be a prudent action.

The Foci of Monitoring

Although identifying and assigning responsibility for monitoring is essential, equally important is the identification of what should be monitored. The work of the group is a chief focus of monitoring. As noted in the previous chapter, monitoring the work progress of the group can be made more effective if measures of success are jointly established by the collaborative team and if milestones and deadlines are communicated in writing to all. These permit the entire team to monitor its progress toward achieving the program vision, and they contribute to a sense of shared leadership and ownership of the group's work.

Development of the relationship must also be constantly monitored. In this case, two aspects are especially important. First, the various tensions identified in the previous chapter must be continually monitored to ensure that an appropriate balance is maintained between them. Second, the developmental processes identified by Ring and Van de Ven (1994) also provide a focus for monitoring the relationship's development. This focus is important for two reasons. A balance between the informal and formal nature of these developmental processes contribute to the balance between several of the tensions identified in Chapter 4 (for example, between formal and informal governance, risk taking and risk avoidance, getting work done, and developing the relationship). In addition, this focus provides more thorough analyses of the various processes of relationship building. In monitoring these, four questions must be asked:

- Is there an appropriate balance between formal bargaining and informal sense making (agreements and understanding reached through interpersonal, social interaction) in the negotiations being conducted as a part of group processes?
- Is there an appropriate balance between formal written agreements and informal ones as a way to ensure the commitment of partner organizations and their representatives to this effort?
- In planning and offering the program, is there an appropriate balance between role interactions (formal coordination of responsibilities assigned to different partners) and interpersonal interactions (informal coordination of responsibilities as partners become more familiar with each other as persons)?
- Is there an appropriate balance between efficiency and equity built into agreements, commitments, and program planning and delivery? Or, is efficiency in governing the relationship and in program planning balanced against an equitable allocation of responsibilities among partners?

Answers to these questions will depend upon how "appropriate balance" is defined for different situations (in the next chapter we will provide guidelines for defining appropriate balance in different programming situations).

Third, the developmental stages of the collaborative relationship must be tracked. Concentrating on these stages helps participants gauge their progress toward developing as a team and accomplishing the tasks associated with each stage. This focus also provides a means through which the pace of relationship development and planning can be assessed, which in turn allows strategy makers and the team as a whole to monitor and establish the preferred pace of development. Finally, the danger signals identified in the previous chapter provide an important focus of monitoring activity. Attending to the presence or absence of these danger signals helps leaders and team members, know whether the relationship remains healthy or is becoming fragile.

Sources of Information

Information about the collaborative effort can come from a variety of sources, including representatives of participating organizations. The wide range of stakeholders in the undertaking, including leaders of organizations and community groups not represented on the team, potential participants in the program, community interest groups, and the media may also serve as information sources.

Effective leaders, the informants pointed out, stay in close touch with a variety of stakeholders to get their impressions of the planning process, program marketing, the program itself, and what should happen next. In fact, leaders and other members of the team may develop a network of stakeholders who are contacted regularly to gather information about perceptions of the collaborative effort. It is essential for this network to include leaders of participating organizations, but it can also be broadened to include others who have a stake in the program.

Potential program participants are also valuable sources of information about the program development process and the program itself. Informants noted the importance of maintaining contact with potential participants in a number of ways, including through informal discussions, updates on progress, periodic assessment of interest and needs as the program begins to unfold, and in meetings with representatives of this group. Informants also highlighted the importance of program evaluations gathered from participants. Although this information is collected after the program has been offered, it still is valuable in providing insights about how the collaborative process and the program itself might be improved.

Other individuals and groups can and do make their feelings heard about collaborative efforts. Some educational programs, particularly those dealing with controversial topics, may draw media attention. These same controversial programs may also bring out special interest groups that want to be sure a certain theme or topic is included or excluded. These groups provide another source of valuable information that can be used in monitoring the effort and anticipating potential problems. In addition, individuals and groups with an interest in and opinion about a collaborative educational program may not always be visible. This is all the more reason for leaders and the major visible stakeholders to look widely for useful opinion.

Monitoring is an essential strategy for sustaining relationships and tracking their development. It is best performed by all members of the collaboration, who gather a variety of information from a variety of sources, both internal and external to the relationship. Monitoring must attend to both the work being accomplished and to the development of the relationship. Failure to monitor either element of collaborative programming may seriously impede progress toward achievement of the program vision, and may in fact allow a relationship to become unnecessarily fragile. But monitoring alone is not enough. It simply provides information that serves as the basis for action.

BUILDING TRUST AND COMMUNICATING

We address trust and communication together because they are so tightly linked and because the informants constantly drew our attention to the relationship between these important components of successful collaboration. Without trust, the quality of communication among partner representatives is weakened. On the other hand, communicating openly, candidly, and frequently with each other helps build the kind of trusting relationship required for a collaborative team to function effectively.

Building Trust

As noted in earlier chapters, the major risk faced in collaboration is the risk to trust. Trust involves one's faith in others' willingness to act with integrity and a sense of moral obligation to the project, the team, and its members. It also involves trusting the competence and capacities of the other organizations and their representatives. In our review of informants' comments, we identified several principles for building trust.

Establishing Norms of Working Together Early in the Process

As the representatives from the staff development organization noted, establishing relationship norms early in the process helps build trusting relationships. Establishment of norms precludes incorrect assumptions and establishes joint expectations for how the group will work together. In addition to norms, it is also helpful to identify the consequences of violating these norms. Although it may be difficult to make these explicit within a group, it is best to discuss them clearly rather than leave them unsaid or misunderstood.

Developing a Vision and Establishing Milestones for Achieving It

Sharing assumptions, interests, and different perspectives as a vision is discussed and developed over time contributes to the building of trust among members. Having a vision also provides a rallying point around which the work of the group can be organized, permitting responsibilities and expectations to be assigned and enthusiasm for work to be fostered. Additionally, having a set of jointly identified milestones helps develop trust. It permits the group to put trust in the competence and capacities of partner organizations and their representatives' ability to fulfill their work obligations and meet deadlines. As the representatives from the staff development organization noted, to generate trust, members of the collaborative effort "must perform." To the extent that partners do perform, trust in these members' competence and capacities is fostered.

It is also necessary, however, for the contributions of participants to be recognized within the group. This process is tied in part to communicating and celebrating small successes, but it goes beyond this. By acknowledging the contributions of individual members and their organizations, the group reinforces trust. This reinforcement strengthens the trust that members have in each other and their social contract by rewarding behavior that fulfills the moral obligations members have to each other. Recognizing the collective impact of individual contributions also reinforces the importance of teamwork and the group's norms for working together.

Having Clear and Visible Support

Leaders of collaborating organizations who provide clear and visible support to the effort also contribute to the development of trust. Obtaining this visible support from partner organizations is again important because it communicates capacity for getting work done. In examples provided by informants, support took the form of funds, staff, facilities, time and energy, expertise, and willingness to champion the effort.

Being Clear About Finances

Clarity about how money is to be spent or shared is critically important to a collaborative relationship. In many ways, this principle is tied to the formal agreements recommended by most informants when finances are involved. The professional association director and the representatives of the staff development organization related experiences in which they were responsible for the budgets of major educational events. Others in the group were very willing to delegate that responsibility to them as long as there was clarity about how finances were to be handled. The procedures employed were adapted to particular demands of the situation and the participating organizations, but in each case there was clarity about these procedures and this clarity contributed to trust among partners.

Standing Together

Standing together is not only a sign of trust but a means for its development. Participants in a collaborative effort come from different organizations to form a temporary one. When these participants report to their superiors and others, they may encounter questions and criticism. As a sign of trust, the informants noted, participants may accept criticism of ideas, but not of people or the importance of working together. By championing the effort collectively, they not only build support for it but contribute to the development of trust within the group.

Compromising

Compromise is rooted in trust. Trusting individuals demonstrate a willingness to act for the collective good, not on the basis of vested interests. This willingness to put individual interests aside for common ones helps develop trust because it demonstrates commitment and obligation to the collaborative effort. Compromise also contributes to group progress, allowing decisions to be made and acted upon efficiently. Compromise is not always possible, but, when it is, acting on this principle contributes to the development of trusting relationships.

Creating Environments for Mutual Benefit

Related to compromising is the need to create a collaborative culture and climate that reinforce the expectation that all partners will benefit from the effort. Such an environment is fostered by using compromise and consensus building as means to make decisions, and abstaining from voting to resolve conflict. In particular, informants advised against voting as a means of decision making. Voting clearly makes some partners winners and others losers, both in terms of individual decisions and possibly for the project as a whole. Acting on the principle of mutual benefit contributes to trust in several ways. It significantly reduces fears that the effort will extract too great a cost from any one partner organization, contributes to positive assessments of equity in the relationship, and focuses on the mutual gains that can be realized from collaborating.

Respecting Others and Developing Friendships

An ingredient in the positive chemistry experienced by the informants in successful collaboration was a form of reinforcement in which all members of the group felt welcome, respected, and valued. Development of this respect apparently occurred through shared compliments and faith in others demonstrated throughout the process. Friendship also enters into this mix and plays an important role. As the professional association director noted, "The fact that we enjoy each other's company can't be undervalued." Mutual respect and friendships may be by-products of previous successful collaboration or they may be developed as the group focuses on the informal nature of the process and the social and psychological contracts that develop among members as they work together. The personal satisfaction of working with others one respects and likes contributes in important ways to building trust.

Building Trust in New Collaborative Ventures

A major challenge in collaboration is building trust among organizations and individuals who are brought together for the first time. In such cases, it is essential that norms related to trust be introduced and addressed immediately. The professional association director also noted that this situation requires those in the convener leadership role to "bend over backwards to demonstrate their trustworthiness." This demonstrates the good faith of the leader and organization bringing the group together. It also models the kinds of behavior that will be required of others to develop the required level of trust. If some members of the group are not totally new to each other, sharing information about previous relationships can be used as a foundation upon which collective trust can be built. In short, these situations call for additional means of building trust, as well as magnified attention to the other principles considered in this section.

Monitoring Trust and Anticipating Problems

Although not addressed directly in our earlier consideration of monitoring, the level of trust in the collaborative relationship requires careful monitoring as well because lack of trust is a key symptom of fragile relationships. Therefore, in any collaborative effort, individuals are well advised to adopt a "what-can-go-wrong" attitude as it relates to trust. This attitude will help draw attention to indicators of trust, as well as to signs that lack of trust is contributing to problems. When it came to trust, the informants strongly suggested constant vigilance. Their experiences indicate that trust is like credit in that it is built slowly but can be destroyed very quickly.

Monitoring trust begins with consideration of the potential chemistry of a group and its likely impact on the level of trust that can be developed. This requires answering questions like the following: How well do collaborators know each other? Have they worked together in the past and, if so, what was the nature of these experiences? In what ways are their organizations complementary? What could lead to disagreements? How much do the leaders of the cooperating organizations support what is to be done? Is the group being forced together by virtue of mandated collaboration, and, if so, what implication does this have for developing trusting relationships? The answers to these questions may provide some sense of how trust will develop among a group of collaborators. They may also predict difficulties that could arise during the course of collaboration.

Once collaboration begins, several of the danger signals identified in the previous chapter become particularly relevant to the issue of trust. Informants specifically identified a failure to communicate with all members of a planning group as one threat to trust. Keeping confidential information in the group is another, while violation of this norm is a clear danger sign. Unilateral decisions that should have been discussed as a group is another symptom of faltering trust. Even well-intentioned enthusiasm to move ahead may lead participants to speak for the group when they have not been approved to do so. Changes in membership also present a possible threat to trust. A group may need to slow down and introduce new members to the norms of the group so that new members know what is expected of them. Although slowing down may stress the effort in other ways, not stopping to attend to the issue of trust as membership changes has much potential for creating even more stress and difficulty. As serious as these threats may be, recognizing them allows the group to effectively confront them.

Communicating

Communication is a major force in building trust, as it is in all facets of collaborative relationships. A few aspects of communication were mentioned a great deal by the informants.

Phatic Communion

As we reviewed informants' comments, they appeared to be discussing an anthropological concept called "phatic communion." This term describes communication usually referred to as "small talk." Phatic communion has several important features which informants highlighted. First, as we have emphasized, there must be elements of both the personal and the professional in collaborative relationships. Time to chat, to engage in small talk is therefore important to developing the personal side of the relationship. This form of communication not only helps in developing the relationship generally, but it also serves to solidify social and psychological contracts and the trust embedded within them. Further, a receptive environment that fosters this form of communication is important, and must be ensured by leaders with the support of all participants in a planning group. As the informants' comments indicated, small talk is necessary before "big talk" in collaboration.

Although phatic communion is essential, so are other forms of communication that focus directly on the work of the group and the relationship itself. Informants offered several principles which guided their practice in this area.

Communicate Frequently and Broadly

Informants agreed that there rarely can be too much communication in collaboration. Representatives of the staff development organization urged individuals planning any kind of partnership to create a broad circle or network of people who are regularly kept informed, and not worry about redundancy. They also suggested that full communication is a fundamental norm for any collaborative effort. Follow-up, especially to keep others informed, is also central to collaboration. As the professional association director noted, "I send information on what we are planning to all those immediately concerned and others who just want to be informed. The cost is minimal and the payoff is very great." Attending to frequent and broad-based communication also contributes to trust. Otherwise, partners and other stakeholders may believe that some are going ahead on their own, undermining the trust that has developed.

Informants also mentioned agendas and other meeting management techniques (for example, sticking to the agenda, summarizing, asking those who speak more to speak less and vice versa) discussed in many publications on the subject. An additional suggestion was to allow enough discussion on the critical items (program focus, specific topics, speakers, and financial matters) for the group to "own" any decision made. Again, the leader and other key participants have to pay attention to the level of ownership, so that any decision will be supported. Although these communication and meeting management techniques will not be elaborated here, they still play a vital role in ensuring that communication among all partners is full and frequent.

Avoid Jargon

Since collaborators come from different organizations, they will have to work hard at avoiding specialized jargon and language that could be confusing. The person leading meetings must ensure that participants understand each other, even if questions are not asked. The need for understanding also calls for leaders and participants to be patient enough to take the time required to foster understanding among members. The practice of asking others if they understand what is being communicated is a simple, but valuable, tool for ensuring that the understanding required in collaboration is achieved.

Use Communication to Develop Shared Meaning

Social interaction through communication is the core process through which meanings are socially constructed and the social and psychological contracts so central to collaboration are formed. This requires more than just ensuring that communication is devoid of confusion. It requires the development of a shared language that captures the meanings embedded in informal contracts and in the group's vision for the program. Therefore, partners have to focus on the language of what is communicated to be certain that meanings are indeed shared.

One challenge associated with having developed a common language and common meaning for working together is the difficulty of sharing this meaning with others in partner organizations. Members of the group must be facile in communicating to both the collaborative relationship and to their own organizations. This skill, as well as the ability to move between these two different settings with ease, is something gained from experience. Yet it is important because it helps to develop the relationship as well as build support for the effort in partner organizations. Therefore, attention to this challenge and even discussion of it will contribute to members' ability to meet it effectively. It is a form of communication that must not be underestimated.

Communicate in Writing

One way to help organizational representatives move successfully between the language cultures of the collaborative relationship and their own organizations is to capture results of discussions and decisions in writing. Whatever is written should both accurately reflect the meanings that have been negotiated and clearly communicate to others outside the group. Written communication does not have to be limited to formal minutes and reports. Rather, it can include memos following discussion of important items, e-mail messages that clarify details of minutes and discussions, and other informal forms of written communication that elaborate on processes and outcomes throughout all stages of collaboration. The principle of frequent and broad communication also pertains to written communication.

Be Candid

Candor and trust are intertwined, with each contributing to the other. The amount of candor possible in a group will be very much a function of the norms established for working together, including the norm of confidentiality for some of the information shared by members. Candor encompasses the willingness to share information that is sensitive, such as information on sponsors who need to be cultivated and the best way to do so, about problems encountered with a speaker, and about partner organizations' evaluations of the effort and the program. Candor also means being up front about information that cannot be shared, providing information circumspectly but being candid that this is being done, and indicating that permission must be garnered before specific information can be shared. Candor is therefore an element of collaboration that has to be worked out by each group for each particular situation.

Use Inclusive Language

The language employed in communication serves important symbolic functions within and outside the collaborative team. As a consequence, it is essential that the language used communicate the collective responsibility and mutual accountability of a collaborative effort. Simply using words like, "team," "ours," and "we," go a long way toward symbolically demonstrating within the group and beyond that partners are working together toward achievement of a shared program vision.

Leadership and Vision in Trust and Communication

Several aspects of leadership and vision mentioned in Chapter 3 are instrumental in creating a climate where trust is possible and clear and frequent communication is the norm. Individuals who perform the convener role must communicate clearly about the potential outcomes of collaborating to attract participants to the effort. In addition, they must be sensitive to a whole host of issues that may affect the level of trust among partners as they first come together. They should be attuned, for example, to asking several of the questions listed earlier for monitoring trust in a collaborative relationship.

Individuals who perform the strategy maker role are at the center of trust building and communication channels once the collaborative effort is underway. They must be sensitive to the need to build a climate where trust is fostered, and act on the principles outlined earlier for doing so. This will entail special attention to the level of trust so that any difficulties that arise can be dealt with quickly. Tactics for intervening will range from confronting the group with the issue so it can deal with it directly, to conversations and even mediation outside of meetings to return trust to an acceptable level. They must ensure that channels of communication are open within the group and to outside decision makers and stakeholders. They must also attend to deadlines and work responsibilities, and recognize and reward the contributions of individuals and the team as a whole so that trust in competencies and capacities is built.

Champions need the information that comes to them through communication channels to act as effective advocates for the program. In addition to being champions of the program, they must also be champions of the relationship. Since one of the central features of effective collaboration is a high degree of trust, they must therefore attend to its development by continually guarding and advocating trust.

Program vision gives the team a focus for its accomplishments, as well as a reason to adhere to the obligations members have to each other. Through the process of vision development, communication is enhanced, shared meaning is negotiated, and opportunities are provided for trust to grow. In addition, a compelling and vital vision acts in its own way as a moral imperative, demanding of partners commitment to work together toward the vision and to engage each other with a shared faith that their mutual moral obligation will remain unaltered. The vision serves, then, as another norm by requiring effective communication, demanding a focus on achieving jointly established milestones, and providing the context within which members' moral obligations to each other are regulated by the social force of having jointly developed and committed to the vision.

Although communicating effectively and building trust are essential, and perhaps the central, strategies for sustaining relationships, there are several others that assist in maintaining relationships. Each requires effective communication and each, if handled well, also contributes to the building of trust.

DEALING WITH DIFFERENCES

By virtue of collaborators coming from several organizations, differences abound in collaboration. These are manifested in the variety of values, philosophies, working norms, and interests representatives and their organizations bring to collaborative efforts. Informants constantly reminded us of this characteristic of collaboration and highlighted several principles they employed in dealing with differences. These included appreciating differences, building consensus, compromising, and developing reciprocal relationships.

Appreciating Differences

Informants noted that differences present themselves in the form of varied competencies, capacities, organizational purposes, mental models, cultures (organizational as well as national), and interests. They provided us with three principles which have helped them appreciate differences. They suggested that it is important to clearly define the strengths of each partner in ways that speak to why the partners are working together. In many respects this principle draws our attention to differences in competencies and capacities, but it also highlights differences in interests, since different interests also serve important purposes in collaboration. Informants also spoke of the need for partners to invest in appreciative processes, or the processes that Gray (1989) defined as including sensitivity to *and* appreciation of differences. As the director of the professional association noted, one of the fastest ways to alienate partners and put stress on trusting relationships is to be insensitive to differences represented in the group. However, the informants reminded us that mere sensitivity to differences is insufficient. They must also be valued for their own sake and on their own terms. Finally, informants reminded us of the need to monitor differences in order to acquire a sensitivity to them as well as gain sufficient understanding and appreciation. As the representative of the consulting firm indicated, partners must take time to understand the values of other organizations—what they are about, how they operate, who to talk to, and their taboos. This final principle again draws our attention to aspects of different organizational culture and the implicit norms and values of organizations and their specialized language. It underscores the need for jargon free communication and hints at a number of principles informants employed when dealing with competing interests.

Core Issues and Interests

Informants repeatedly reminded us that the presence of competing interests is an inherent characteristic of collaboration. Organizations and individuals are drawn to the effort because they have interests in the program but their interests are not necessarily the same. The representatives of the staff development organization highlighted a critical principle for dealing with these different interests, both initially and throughout the collaborative process—the need to separate interests from personalities and events. They noted that we too often define problems in terms of personalities or events rather than focus on the causes of the challenges that confront the collaborative effort.

The principle these informants have recommended captures the essence of several strategies for "principled" or "win-win" bargaining advanced by Fisher and Ury (1981). Principled bargaining is centered around four strategies—(a) separating people (and also events in our case) from the problem, (b) focusing on interests instead of positions, (c) inventing options for mutual gain, and (d) insisting on objective standards for fairness both in substance and negotiating procedures.

Focusing on issues and the interests associated with them opens up many more avenues for addressing and managing differences than those provided by focusing only on events or personalities. In an earlier chapter we reported that one of our informants had at times replaced members of a group if they lacked commitment or failed to deliver on their responsibilities. However, taking this action on the basis of personality or an individual's behavior would be accompanied by several risks. One risk is assuming that the organization represented by the individual is uninterested in the program. On the contrary, a focus on interests might show that the organizational partner is interested, although its representative is not. In this case the wise course of action would be to replace the individual with a more committed and interested individual from the same organization. A focus on interests might also indicate that the behaviors observed stem from the fact that planning has overlooked the organization's or representative's interests. Allowing time for the representative to express these interests, and addressing them openly within the collaborative group may not only increase the motivation of this partner but also contribute to the health of the relationship. Finally, a focus on interests creates opportunities for using the strategies of consensus and compromise to deal with differences in creative and effective ways.

Consensus

Informants avoided voting in decision making because it results in labeling partners as winners or losers, effectively dividing the group into camps. Informants instead encouraged individuals engaged in collaboration to use consensus for decision making. The director of the professional association and the representatives from the staff development organization noted that when conflicting interests (for example, about topics to be included in a program) resulted in stalemate, they either dropped the issue or helped the group come up with a novel, consensual solution that addressed each conflicting interest, thus allowing maintenance of each organization's position. As a consequence, another benefit was realized: Definitions of problems or solutions were generated that would not have been possible if differences were either ignored or addressed in less than productive ways. The director of the local government education program also pointed out that consensus building often takes place outside meetings where leaders have conversations with and mediate among members with competing interests. Using a consensual model of decision making also helped partners avoid having to deal with issues and battles that detracted from the purpose of collaboration and would be more appropriately relegated to other venues for resolution. A focus on consensus, then, requires recognition that different interests exist within any collaborative arrangement and that there are no shortcuts for dealing with them. Rather, achieving consensus requires flexibility and creativity of leaders and members alike in order to deal with differences constructively and reap the rewards of doing so.

Compromise

Consensus cannot be reached unless partners are willing to compromise. One informant noted that, "collaboration virtually requires compromise and is enhanced by it." Other informants suggested that compromise requires partners to put aside their vested interests and refrain from dominating the process so that the common interests are met. In making this recommendation, they reminded us that the program being planned is far more important than the vested interests of individual representatives and organizations. They also noted that compromise requires that all partners participate, contribute, and have a fair hearing. Otherwise, their interests remain unknown to the group and cannot be addressed in the processes of compromise and consensus building.

But informants also reminded us that there are both costs and limits to compromise. A cost of compromise is loss of control of an organization's agenda. Compromise always extracts this cost, so the issue becomes how much individuals and organizations are willing to compromise in order to reach consensus and move the collaborative arrangement forward. Informants suggested three major principles for dealing with this issue. First, it is essential to recognize that there will be limits to compromise. These limits usually revolve around the need to maintain individual and organizational integrity, and the need to avoid subversion of program vision and goals. As the director of the professional association noted, "While compromise is important, you must maintain, not subvert, your own integrity to satisfy others, even if this endangers future collaboration." His association's year-long debate with a trade association illustrates this principle in practice. Neither the professional association nor the trade association was willing to compromise on its basic principles and interests. Discussion eventually ended, but with each organization's integrity intact. This result may have endangered future collaboration between the two organizations but, by maintaining the integrity of each, it may have also built a foundation for future collaboration.

Second, it is important to lay out the boundaries of compromise (organizational needs, policies, procedures) in the beginning of the collaborative effort. Providing an opportunity for each partner to communicate its boundaries for compromise establishes another norm for working together. These norms become part of the informal, social contract of the group and establish the parameters within which formal bargaining can occur. The establishment of these norms strikes a balance between sense making and bargaining in the negotiation developmental process identified by Ring and Van de Ven (1994).

Third, it is crucial to document and communicate compromises to all stakeholders. Representatives of the staff development organization document compromises reached in decision making to guard against representatives of partner organizations either feeling hurt or being punished for compromising when they return to their own organizations. Documentation and communication in this instance serve two purposes: They provide an avenue for the group to recognize compromise as a form of contributing to the effort and communicate compromise to important stakeholders as contributions rather than as capitulation to other organizations' individual vested interests.

Building Reciprocal Relationships

Related to differences is the need to attend to the cultivation of others. In many respects, this principle returns us to consideration of reciprocity, or the diffuse obligation one person or organization feels to another person or organization. By being candid, sharing information in a timely way, thanking people for their contributions, compromising, being willing to change, and developing a program that will be valued by all partners, reciprocity is developed with others within and beyond the collaborative group. This cultivation of others, or building a sense of reciprocity among organizational representatives, their organizations' leaders, and other stakeholders, contributes much to the effectiveness of collaboration. It contributes to relationship building and develops a foundation for dealing with differences more effectively.

Managing differences and issues is an important strategy in sustaining and building relationships. It requires attention to consensual decision-making processes, the art and limits of compromise, appreciative processes, and the development of reciprocity among partners. Although these principles of collaborative program planning are required during active collaboration, they also contribute to the development of long-term relationships that, while at times relatively inactive, can nonetheless be drawn upon when collaborative opportunities present themselves. In fact, the importance of relative inactivity or "rest" in collaboration, as well as the pace of growth in programming are important considerations for those who undertake collaborative projects.

RESTING AND GROWING

Setting the pace of collaboration is an important task of the strategy maker leadership role. The amount of "rest" or "down time" built into the process, and the speed at which collaborators permit the program(s) being planned and offered to grow in complexity are two key elements of successful pacesetting.

Rest can be considered from two major perspectives. The first relates to need for building sufficient time into the collaborative effort so participants can fulfill responsibilities at their home organizations, have opportunities to step back from the strain of working with others, reflect on what has been accomplished, and consider next steps. This perspective draws our attention again to the cost of time in collaboration and to the recognition that those who participate in collaboration tend to be busy people who have other responsibilities. Sufficient "down time" must therefore be built into the collaborative process so that time and energy are not too quickly drained and participants have time to reflect on what they have done before moving forward. Building in this kind of "resting" time may be accomplished by having fewer meetings, by focusing efforts on a priority collaborative program so that participants' efforts can be concentrated on it rather than being diffused among several, and delegating program details to staff and partner organizations that have more than sufficient capacity to deal with them. Informants, especially the park district manager and the professional association director, highlighted these strategies for providing "rest" within the context of the intensity that is so characteristic of collaboration.

The second perspective on "rest" is the need for collaborators to take time out from collaboration once the program has been offered. Again, given the intensity of collaborating, time away from partners once a collaborative project is completed provides opportunities to recover from the costs of energy and time committed to it so that capacity is renewed for future efforts. Although collaborators are not engaged with each other at this time, this does not mean that relationships are broken. Rather, they are just dormant. These relationships may be drawn upon again when future collaborative opportunities present themselves. Thus, rest, both during collaborative efforts and between them offers important opportunities to renew and reflect.

Another element of pacing is the rapidity with which the collaborative team permits a program or several programs to grow in complexity. Sometimes complexity occurs unexpectedly as a result of changes in the external environment. The rapid and unanticipated growth of the park district's program is one example of this type of growth. In other instances, the collaborative effort will be complex from the very beginning. The staff development organization's programs that focus on systemic change and the cohort graduate program of collaborating universities illustrate this type of program. Yet, both simple programs and more complex ones can still become more complicated. Three examples from the informants' experience illustrate this point.

- In the park district, small educational programs for the general community held at one site were taken to additional ones, with more sessions added, because of the interest shown in them. Schools, senior citizen centers, and other non-park locations were used for these programs.
- The international seminar program of the professional association has grown progressively larger, entering regions of the world where scientists had not had access to valuable information on recent research findings. The number of trade associations willing to support these programs has also increased over time. Not only has the number of partners increased in these efforts, but the intricacies of offering programs in diverse parts of the world have made these offerings increasingly complex.
- The educational and service program for local government officials began to serve a statewide audience in the second year of its operation. Distance learning technologies were used to reach audiences throughout the state, with audio- and videoconferencing added over time, as support for these additions was garnered from partners.

In these and other examples provided by informants, slow growth was evident. Informants chose an incremental approach to increasing the complexity and scope of collaboration and programs. They used lessons learned from each collaborative program iteration as bases for deciding how quickly programs and the collaborative relationship could grow in complexity. In contrast to pacing that occurs within a single collaborative effort, this form of pacing is related to program growth over extended periods of time. By taking time to "rest" and by growing incrementally, informants were able to control the level of stress in the relationship, garner support for growing in complexity and scope, provide time for the collaborative effort to solidify as changes were made, and offer opportunities for reflection and assessment of next steps.

DEVELOPING EFFECTIVE TEAMWORK

As we reflected on informant interviews and the literature of collaboration, we found a great deal of consistency between the themes identified for sustaining and developing relationships and recommendations for developing and supporting high performing teams. Katzenbach and Smith (1993) have defined a team as " . . . a small group of people with complementary skills who are committed to a common purpose, set of performance goals, and approach for which they hold themselves mutually accountable" (p. 112). They have also noted that teams are characterized by shared leadership, open-ended discussion and problem-solving meetings, joint decision making and work, positive recognition and feedback, and psychological bonding (Katzenbach & Smith, 1993). Each of these elements has been addressed previously. The importance of shared leadership roles and a common vision or purpose was introduced in Chapter 1 and elaborated in Chapter 3. In Chapter 4 we highlighted the importance of team size and the mix of complementary skills and expertise. In this and previous chapters, we have drawn attention to jointly determined milestones and mutual accountability for reaching them. We have also illustrated, through informants' examples, the importance of recognizing and rewarding small successes, making decisions in a consensual manner, the importance of social and psychological contracts, and the intensity and time required in working together.

Collaboration is therefore a form of teamwork that is developed through attention to all the processes and tensions introduced so far. However, it is a special type of teamwork that develops among people from several organizations that differ in important ways. Therefore a team of individuals from different organizations is both like and unlike a team of individuals from the same organization. Many of the processes required for high performing teams are the same, as the consistency of themes noted above demonstrates. But the special motivations for interorganizational team formation, the temporary nature of collaborative relationships, their unconventional governance, the degree of balance required among a variety of competing tensions, and the fact that members come to the team from different organizations, magnifies the importance of the strategies that have been reviewed, adds subtle, but important, dimensions to the strategies, and complicates the means and ease with which strategies can be carried out. Insights about teamwork in single organizations provide a necessary, but insufficient basis, for understanding effective teamwork in interorganizational collaboration. Other elements, such as balance among competing tensions, unconventional governance and leadership, and differences in fundamental interests demand attention as strategies are chosen and implemented. The temporary nature of collaboration also requires special attention, because unlike teams within a single organization which may be required to produce a product before disbanding, collaborative teams may become fragile and dissolve prior to implementing programs.

DEALING WITH FRAGILE RELATIONSHIPS

Once signs of fragility are identified, three major options are available.

Doing Nothing

First, a decision can be made to do nothing about the increasingly fragile situation. Two possibilities may result from such an approach. The collaborative effort may continue intact, though tenuous, until the program is complete. By taking this stance, program outcomes may be less than optimal because the fragility of the relationship was left unaddressed. In addition, if collaboration ends having produced a product but without having dealt with a relationship's fragility and the issues that created it, the potential for future collaboration may be seriously reduced. Another potential outcome of doing nothing is that the relationship will simply end. Participants may fail to attend meetings and communications may cease, leading to the collapse of the relationship. In this case, the potential for harm to future collaboration is very great. The collaboration has been unsuccessful, partners may leave with ill feelings about others, and norms may have been violated so much that little can be done to repair them. The chance for this same group of organizations to collaborate again has been greatly diminished. Given these possible outcomes, a decision to do nothing in the face of danger signals would appear to be unwise.

Saving the Relationship

Most collaborators, fortunately, have two other options. One is to make an effort to salvage the relationship. The other is to deliberately and systematically dissolve it. Saving a relationship is the more difficult of the two. As the informants pointed out, rescuing a collaborative relationship calls for levels of effort, candor, and diplomacy that may be difficult to reach. Leaders and major stakeholders are critically important to this process. They will have to recognize that conditions have changed and plan an agenda for discussing what must be done to keep the group intact. This process also requires careful identification and definition of problems associated with danger signals. It requires judicious selection of strategies for dealing with the problems that have been identified. In addition, depending on the situation, team members or leaders will have to make decisions about whether to employ these strategies within the group, outside the group with individual participants, or in some combination. The problem, characteristics of the collaborative effort, the strategy itself, and the understanding gained through monitoring the relationship will have much bearing on selecting and employing an appropriate strategy.

Monitoring the relationship and the work of the team is central to obtaining early warning signs that problems are developing. The earlier problems are identified the greater the likelihood for salvaging the relationship. If monitoring reveals minor or moderate problems, then the relationship is probably worth rescuing. If problems are serious—if there is evidence of irreconcilable differences in interests or a feeling that trust has been irreparably destroyed—then dissolving the relationship may be the only option.

However, the decision to salvage a relationship or dissolve it is possible only if organizations have voluntarily agreed to collaborate. In mandated collaboration the number of options is reduced. In short-term contractual agreements, a decision can be made either to salvage the relationship, or to do nothing more than fulfill contractual obligations and let the effort end. The former option is of course the best, since it improves the chances of the same organizations collaborating again. But, if the relationship cannot be salvaged, it may just have to run its course with the consequence of a reduced prospect of future collaboration. The consulting firm's experience with the government agency is a case in point.

Situations in which collaboration is required over a long period of time, such as one mandated by law, pose even more challenges since failing to salvage relationships in these situations raises the specter of misery for the duration of the endeavor. Doing nothing in this situation is certainly an option. But, given the long-term psychological costs of refraining from action, salvaging the relationship with remedial action would be the better of the two strategies. Again, monitoring the situation, defining problems, and selecting associated strategies are keys to salvaging a relationship. As we have noted, mandated collaboration does not necessarily mean that the relationship will be poor or unproductive. Rather, mandated collaboration creates special circumstances (for example, competing organizations working together when they would otherwise not choose to do so) that frame and constrain how various strategies that have been suggested can be employed. These constraints do not mean that the strategies will not work. Rather, to work, the strategies will have to be adapted to the unique circumstances of mandated efforts. They are certainly worth trying, given the costs of failure. The example provided by the distance education consortium, a voluntary collaborative effort within a mandated one, illustrates this point. By voluntarily collaborating within a mandated situation, the participating institutions created ways to build trust, solve problems, and keep the stresses of mandated collaboration at as low a level as possible.

Dissolving the Relationship

In voluntary collaboration, dissolving the relationship is always possible. A decision to dissolve a relationship is usually made if the relationship itself has been irreversibly harmed, if the work of the collaborative effort has completely stalled, or if the program being planned is no longer feasible. If progress is not being made and cannot be made for a variety of reasons, dissolving the relationship may be the optimal decision. It may be decided that the program being planned is no longer a possibility, and, again, this most likely calls for a dissolution. Finally, if a purpose no longer exists for collaboration, even though the group works well together and members like each other, this may also call for dissolution. However, as Ring and Van de Ven (1994) have noted, collaborative groups often have difficulty disbanding in these circumstances. Members' psychological contracts may have become so strong that disbanding creates emotional discomfort for them, even in cases in which no additional work needs to be accomplished. The park district manager related that at one meeting of a collaborative effort all participants agreed that the group had outlived its usefulness. Although this group could find no purpose or program that would fit the current composition of the group, the members still had difficulty disbanding because they liked each other and had collaborated effectively. However, the group did dissolve with strong relationships intact, and the participants have worked together again.

Dissolving a relationship is a difficult process, even under the best of circumstances. Informants recommended strongly that groups be dissolved deliberately and systematically, with the maximum amount of professionalism possible. In addition, informants suggested that dissolution be discussed forthrightly, with particular attention being paid to what the group has accomplished, why it has chosen to disband, and what circumstances have led to the end of the collaborative effort. The processes and tensions of collaboration covered in earlier chapters provide valuable insights for understanding the various circumstances that have led to dissolution. Explicitly discussing these factors has an added benefit. It serves as a form of evaluation for the collaborative process and contributes to an increased understanding of the dynamics of collaborative work on the part of all participants. These strategies create the conditions required for participants to want to work together again when circumstances permit.

Dissolution may require other arrangements to be made. Formal contracts and informal agreements may have to be voided. If finances are involved, agreement must be reached about sharing expenses and/or income. If items were purchased, decisions must be made about who will use them. Accommodations also may have to be made for storing the records of the group, so they can be accessed again when similar efforts begin. Finally, rites of mourning may be required. These rites offer a venue for celebrating what has been accomplished, contribute to any healing that may be needed, and help people let go of the past and look to the future (Bolman & Deal, 1997). Mourning the end of collaborative relationships is especially important owing to the social and psychological contracts that have been formed and the meaning that has been socially constructed through interaction of participants. These rites provide people with ways to transition out of intense relationships to which they have contributed much.

Dealing with fragile relationships requires careful monitoring, consideration of danger signals and the problems that underlie them, and judicious selection among a variety of strategies for saving the relationship. But the existence of fragile relationships also raises the specter of the need to end them. Dissolution requires a great deal of deliberate and careful planning and professionalism so that possibilities for future collaboration are not affected any more negatively than necessary. Dissolution also requires attention to a number of final arrangements and the provision of transition rites to help participants let go of the past and invest in the future.

CONCLUSION

There is an assumption in the literature that, once started, collaborative relationships just naturally continue. We have addressed the inaccuracy of this implicit assumption by highlighting the ceaseless and sophisticated work required of all partners for collaborative relationships to be maintained. In fact, the information provided by informants suggests that there actually may be more work associated with maintaining a collaborative relationship than with starting one.

We have repeatedly noted that the balances between tensions in collaboration and the strategies employed to keep relationships "in suitable condition" are very much a function of each specific situation. The situation for collaboration is defined both by the complexity and scope of programming and the intensity of collaboration required for different program efforts.

CHAPTER 6

Assessing Collaborative Relationships

The practitioners from whom we have drawn examples and insights for this book represent a variety of organizations and practice settings. They provided many different examples of programs they have planned and offered through collaboration. These programs ranged in complexity and scope from simple, one-event programs whose purpose was the provision of information, to major efforts composed of multiple educational events aimed at systemic change. As we compared informants' discussion of their collaborative practices with the range of programs they described, it became evident that the intensity and intricacies of collaboration varied with the scope and complexity of programs. In short, not all programmatic efforts require the same levels of intensity.

How does one decide upon the level of collaboration required for different programs? In this chapter we address this question in three ways. First, we suggest a continuum of program complexity, characterized across several dimensions, against which the scope and complexity of programming can be assessed. Then, we discuss several guidelines that can be used to decide upon the intensity of collaboration required for programs at various places on the complexity continuum. Finally, we provide a list of guiding questions that can be used to assess collaborative efforts. These questions can be used for planning, for formative evaluation, and for summative evaluation.

THE RELATION BETWEEN PROGRAM COMPLEXITY AND COLLABORATIVE INTENSITY

Cervero (1988, 1992) has chosen to cast collaboration within a framework of interdependence among organizations. The first four orientations of the six in his typology of organizational interdependence—monopoly, parallelism, and competition, and cooperation—were beyond the scope of this book. However, his description and definition of the last two orientations, coordination, and, especially collaboration, provided one theoretical foundation for our understanding of collaboration in program planning and delivery. Examples of each of these categories also came from informants. The distance education consortium was primarily a coordinative effort since institutions developed a process, within the context of mandated collaboration, to coordinate their programs rather than compete. Other examples given by informants were primarily collaborative in that, at minimum, their programs were cosponsored by several different organizations.

Cervero (1988, 1992) has indicated that the different categories of organizational interdependence are discrete. However, our data, like Tallman's (1990), pointed instead to variation across and within these categories based upon the intensity of the relationship, or interdependence, among partner organizations. Intensity, in this case, is defined as the amount of investment each organization makes in the risks and benefits of the collaborative effort. Although the distance education consortium could be classified as a coordinative effort, it was nonetheless a relationship in which many dynamics of collaborative work were found. Issues of balance between formal and informal governance processes, of communication and trust, and of ways to relieve stress in the relationship were evident in this effort. Variation was also found in relationships that could be classified as collaborative. The intensity with which short, informational programs were planned by the park district differed from the level of intensity required by this same organization to plan and adapt to the major community program that unexpectedly grew very large. Examples of systemic change programming provided by representatives of the staff development organization illustrated situations in which an even higher level of intensity was required. Collaborative planning of programs that last a short period of time and reach a small audience will not need to be approached with the same level of intensity as ones that are broader in scope and more complex. Therefore, programs do vary on the basis of their complexity, and having a way to assess this level of complexity provides guidance about the intensity of collaboration required to plan and offer them.

Program Complexity and Scope

The literature on program planning in adult and continuing education provides some guidance on how different kinds of programs can be categorized on the basis of their complexity and scope. Boyle (1981), for example, has identified three kinds of programs—developmental, institutional, and informational. Developmental programs are focused on helping people address and/or cope with societal problems. Institutional programs, in contrast, provide content that will enable individuals to improve their skills and abilities. Informational programs provide and explain information for learners across a range of issues. Generally, developmental programs are the most complex, followed by institutional and then informational programs. Boyle (1981) also identified a category of programs that he has labeled, "major change programs." Major change programs incorporate a series of related activities that are directed toward resolution of major problems. This category of program is also characterized by a large number of activities (or discrete, smaller programs), extensive use of resources, and the large numbers of people who plan the program and are affected by it. The systemic change initiatives planned collaboratively by the staff development organization are examples of this category of program.

Houle (1996) has argued that collaborative efforts can be

analyzed in terms of three basic dimensions—(a) the number of partner organizations involved, (b) the different kinds of contributions made by partners, and (c) the complexity of interaction between partners. The three dimensions identified by Houle (1996), as well as insights from Boyle (1981), have been included in the continuum of program complexity and scope we have developed.

Continuum of Program Complexity and Scope

We have developed a three-category typology of program complexity and scope. Categories in this typology are broadly defined and are viewed as existing on a continuum from lower to increased complexity. We do not consider the categories to be discrete ones. With change in a few dimensions, a fairly simple program can easily become moderately complex. In addition, some programs will share different dimensions of complexity. A program may be characterized as being of low complexity with respect to the number of programming details that demand attention, but at the same time be complex with regard to an ill-defined problem domain and/or conflict of interests among collaborators.

Each category has been identified and defined using several characteristics (for example, program duration, planning complexity, diversity and nature of organizational interests) related to the programs themselves, their planning, and related elements of collaboration. The characteristics employed in developing this typology have been derived from interview data from informants, our own experiences with collaborative programming, and the literature on program planning. The three categories are (a) programs of low complexity and limited scope, (b) programs of moderate complexity and scope, and (c) programs of high complexity and broad scope. This categorization, we believe, is a new contribution to practice-based thinking regarding the relation between collaboration and program development.

Programs of Low Complexity and Limited Scope

Easily planned and operated adult and continuing education programs, which have a very simple format, generally require less intense collaboration than more complex ones. This is especially true when these programs have been held on many previous occasions and are well supported by the cosponsors. The programs of the park district, professional association, staff development organization, and local government training program provided examples of such programs which shared the following characteristics:

- The topic for the program is narrow and clearly defined and the problem domain addressed by the program is well-defined.
- The audience for the program is well-defined and relatively small. Participants will likely attend the program because its benefit is clear.
- The program is short, being offered for a limited number of days or sessions.
- The amount of detail required to plan and offer the program is limited. As a consequence, the planning time is short, requiring perhaps only one meeting, or two to three at most over a relatively short period of time.
- The financial investment and potential income are limited and probably will not be shared among partner organizations. Rather, only one organization will be responsible for finances and taking financial risks.
- Accountability for the program is limited, with few if any formal evaluations or reports required.
- Collaborators have a good history of working together. If programming involves new collaborators, both the time required for planning and the clear focus on the topic and problem domain will reduce the possibility of personnel changing or encountering serious disagreements.
- Collaborators have limited investment of time and energy in the planning of the program.
- Collaborators' interests in the program are relatively similar and/or the program addresses a topic within collaborating or-

ganizations' "zones of indifference" (areas where interests have limited bearing or are not at stake). The program is of sufficient interest to engender collaboration and cosponsorship, but does not threaten important interests of the parties involved.

In this type of program, the collaborators might provide suggestions at one meeting and leave the details to staff members of the major partner. The collaborators are kept informed of progress, but the program may not be a high priority among other programs or areas they are addressing. In some instances, the informants reported, these programs were part of a larger ongoing collaborative effort, and a demonstration that different groups would work together. Although the programs took little time to plan and were quickly over, their individual success added to the strength of ongoing reciprocal relationships. And despite their relative simplicity, these programs still require understanding of and attention to the principles discussed in this book.

Programs of Moderate Complexity and Scope

Programs of moderate complexity require more attention and involvement by collaborators. However, they too may have certain characteristics which limit the intensity needed in collaboration. These programs also may be characterized by a history that includes the same partner organizations participating in planning the program. Multiple meetings over a period of weeks or months will be required for planning. The program offered may be a conference or seminar that lasts several days and may require increased attention to performance of all leadership roles, the input of a planning committee, the sharing of information and different perspectives, and attention to the strains on collaboration. The following characteristics are common in programs of moderate complexity:

- The program's topic is relatively diffuse, and may include treatment of a variety of areas and the introduction of controversial matters. The problem domain addressed by the program is moderately well-defined.

- The potential participant audience is loosely defined, perhaps as a result of the program being new, the topic being more diffuse, or the program being of widespread interest. The number of program participants is relatively large.
- The program is longer, lasting several days, with several activities going on simultaneously.
- The amount of detail required in planning and implementing the program is moderate, owing to the length of the program, audience size and diversity, multiple sessions, and diffuse nature of topics covered. Planning for the program occurs over an extended period of time, perhaps up to six months.
- Fiscal risk will be shared by more than one partner organization.
- Accountability for the program is moderate, with several stakeholders who need to be kept informed of progress and the results.
- Because the length of planning time is extended, the chance of personnel change is increased. In addition, the diffuse nature of topics and the relative ambiguity of the problem domain pose increased challenges for working with organizations that have not been part of previous collaborative efforts.
- Each partner invests considerable time and energy to the success of the program.
- Partner organizations attach distinct political importance to the program, since their varied interests are at stake.

All of these characteristics add elements of risk to the program and the collaborative effort. Leaders, especially those performing the convener and strategy maker roles, must be respected and trusted by all involved in the program. Because the planning process may be a long one, those making decisions must be kept fully informed and must support the directions being taken. Relationships, along with program management, must be primary concerns. Each of the informants described programs that fit into this category. They typically emerged as the group became more comfortable working together, more candid about the need for certain educational programs, and more willing to take calculated risks.

Programs of High Complexity and Broad Scope

Highly complex programs require a high level of intensity in collaboration. Most informants identified programs that required this level of intensity. The park district annually held a large recreational event for the entire community. The international professional association sponsored an annual conference for all of its members in different parts of the world. The staff development organization was the recipient of a grant for a major new educational effort involving many educational and social service organizations in its community. The local government education program participated in annual state conferences on economic development. The statewide graduate program required a high level of intense collaboration among all participating institutions. The consulting firm was involved in a number of programs requiring long-term collaboration on the part of governmental agencies, professional associations, and a host of other organizations. Such highly complex programs are characterized by the following:

- The program's topic is very broad and complex. The problem domain addressed by the program is very vague and ill-defined. Therefore, defining the problem and developing a clear program vision for addressing it takes a great deal of time and effort.
- The potential audience is a large, very diverse, and loosely defined group, represented by a variety of potential partner organizations.
- Program length will vary from a long traditional program to months and years in a major change program.
- The planning, management, and operation of the program are highly complex and have to be orchestrated so the diverse organizations involved achieve harmony instead of dissonance. The time required for planning is therefore long, lasting for more than six months.

- A great deal of money that could be spent and lost, or spent with a healthy return on the investment, is involved for most partner organizations.
- The level of accountability required is great, with many stakeholders who have to be kept informed, whose questions have to be answered, and whose approval is a necessity.
- Because the length of planning time required is extensive, the chance of personnel change within the collaborative relationship is markedly increased.
- The diffuse nature of program topics and the ill-defined problem domain pose many challenges for working with organizations that have not been part of previous collaborative efforts.
- Collaborators make extensive investments of time and energy in the planning of the program.
- Partner organizations' interests in the program are diverse so the possibility that vested interests will complicate planning is increased. For risks and benefits to be balanced, all partner organizations have to find the program of value.
- Decisions have increased potential for creating "winners" and "losers." Therefore, difficulties at arriving at consensus and compromise are probable.

These programs put the greatest demands on partners but can be the flagship efforts of collaboration.

Using the Continuum

These three program types are on a continuum upon which programs vary in their complexity and scope across the various characteristics. The three levels of program complexity are broad ones indeed. A list of all possible types of programs would be difficult to assemble and analyze. Although pure program types will exist, most programs will be characterized by mixtures of the various characteristics and will be placed on different points of the continuum. A program may have a relatively clear topic and potential audience, require little planning time and attention to detail owing to its relatively short duration, but also require sharing of financial risks among several organizations and a relatively high level of accountability, especially for finances. In this instance the program would be placed on the continuum between programs of limited complexity and programs of moderate complexity. Therefore, the continuum, and the various characteristics that have led to its definition, is to be used as a subjective guide in assessing the level of program complexity and scope and determining the intensity of collaboration required.

In general, as programs become more complex and broader in scope, collaborators will have to attend more to the various tensions identified in Chapter 4, and to ensuring balance between formal and informal governance structures. Increased complexity also results in increased risks to trust, equity, and reciprocity, and these risks in particular must increasingly be the focus of attention. The roles of leadership and vision addressed in Chapter 3 and the various strategies for balancing tensions highlighted in Chapters 4 and 5 also become increasingly important as programs become more complex.

A very simple program can be planned with little attention to balance. It might be planned in a very formal way, with professional roles dominating, or very informally, especially if partner organizations have collaborated before. This is possible because the program and its planning are simple, one organization will probably take most financial risks, and the program addresses a topic in collaborating organizations' zones of indifference. In stark contrast, programs of high complexity and broad scope by definition require intense collaboration.

Programs of moderate complexity and scope are the most difficult to assess in terms of the intensity of collaboration required. This is the case because they vary so much across the various characteristics. In fact, they are the "mine fields" of collaboration. They may present themselves as relatively simple, lulling collaborators into thinking that few tensions will exist, little attention to balance will be required, and few risks will be taken. They may nevertheless contain sufficient complexity to call for intense collaboration. If they are not approached with this understanding, collaborators may quickly begin to experience difficulties they have not anticipated. These programs are more likely than the other two to be transformed, either into simpler or more complex programs. Consequently, monitoring and anticipating changes in these programs is critical. In addition, it is wise to enter the planning of moderately complex programs expecting that the intensity of collaboration will be high. Relaxing one's guard once it is determined that the intensity required is lower than expected is always easier than dealing with problems that occur because they are unanticipated.

Assessing the complexity and scope of programs provides a basis, then, for anticipating the intensity of collaboration needed in their planning and implementation. The continuum and the various characteristics identified for each program type also provide an additional focus for monitoring collaborative programming. By attending to changes in a program, the possibilities for accurately matching the intensity of collaboration required with programs of different complexity are likewise increased. To be effective, however, attention must be paid to the various programmatic and collaborative elements addressed in this and earlier chapters.

ASSESSING THE RELATIONSHIP BETWEEN PROGRAM COMPLEXITY AND INTENSITY OF COLLABORATION

Grotelueschen (1980) has noted that evaluation can be used prior to a program for planning purposes, during a program for formative purposes, and at a program's end in a summative way. We believe the same approach should be employed in evaluating collaborative efforts. As guides to developing evaluations of these efforts, we have distilled a series of questions from the information obtained from informants, from the literature, and from our own experiences. The questions are not intended for use as elements of an all-purpose, comprehensive evaluation instrument. We have purposefully made them broad so they can be adapted to different circumstances. We begin with a series of questions that can be used to identify a program's scope and complexity and place it on the complexity continuum. Then, we provide a series of questions about the collaborative relationship itself. These remaining questions are organized around the themes of Chapters 3, 4 and 5 and are intended for use in assessing the strength and intensity of the relationship.

Program Complexity and Scope

- How narrow/broad and clearly defined is the program topic?
- Is the problem domain well-defined, moderately well-defined, or ill-defined?
- How well-defined is the potential program audience?
- What is the anticipated size of the audience?
- What is the anticipated duration of the program?
- What is the anticipated duration of planning?
- What level of detail is required to plan and offer the program?
- What is the level of financial risk, and to what extent is it to be shared?
- What is the required level of accountability, and which stakeholders have to be kept informed about the collaborative effort and its outcomes?
- To what extent do collaborators have a history of working together? What are the probabilities for change in personnel during planning and implementation?
- What investment of time and energy is required of collaborators?
- How diverse and vested are the interests of collaborators?

Leadership and Vision

- What collaborative leadership roles are required? Who is performing the roles and why?
- To what extent is leadership shared?
- How effectively and intensely are the roles being performed?
- Are leaders visible or are they acting behind the scenes? Why?
- How well are leaders dealing with risks, communication, conflict, and unexpected developments?

- How are leaders monitoring work and motivating others to meet deadlines?
- How are they monitoring and attending to the development of the relationship?
- How are they contributing to the development of the program vision?
- Who is most responsible for developing the vision?
- How much time is it taking to develop the vision? Why?
- To what extent is the vision addressing the collaborators' differences? What impact is this having on the relationship?
- Is the vision clear and compelling?
- Is the vision clear enough so that it can be used throughout the planning process? Can it be modified? Does it have to be modified? Why?
- Is the vision a factor in motivating the planning group? Is it being used as a planning guide? If so, how and why is it being used? If not, why not?
- What is the vision contributing to the planning process?
- Is the vision clear enough to be easily understood by potential participants in the program?
- How well is the vision matching what is actually being planned?
- Does the vision address the outcome of developing a long-term relationship among collaborators? Why or why not?

Tensions

- What are the tensions in the relationship?
- How well are these tensions being handled?
- How is the tension between having a vision and the process of developing vision being handled?
- How formal or informal is the group's governance? Is there an appropriate and effective balance between the formal and the informal? How is the pattern of governance impacting the group's effectiveness?
- Is the emphasis on accomplishment interfering with relationship building or vice versa? If so, in what ways?
- Are risks being taken? What kind and by whom? What is happening as a result?

- Is the group being transformed in any way during the planning process? Is the transformation positive or negative? How are transformations being monitored and dealt with?
- In what, if any, way is the collaborative effort being put in danger?

Strategies

- Who is monitoring the relationship and its work?
- How is monitoring being conducted? What sources of information are being tapped? Are all the elements being monitored? Why or why not? How effective is the monitoring?
- How is trust being built among partners?
- Are explicit norms established for working together?
- Are other strategies for building trust being used? Why or why not?
- Is special attention being paid to building trust in new collaborative ventures or in ones in which several collaborators are new?
- Is trust being monitored? By whom is it being monitored and how?
- How effective, frequent, and complete is communication?
- What communication problems must be overcome? Why?
- How candid are participants at the outset of planning and as planning continues?
- How effectively is information being shared to stakeholders outside the planning team?
- Is the level of understanding among collaborators high? Why or why not?
- To what extent are collaborators understanding and valuing their several differences?
- Is the group focusing on core issues and interests rather than on personalities and events? Why or why not?
- Are consensus and compromise being used? Are limits to compromise clearly articulated and understood by the group?
- Is attention being paid to the need for cultivating others and building reciprocal relationships?
- Does the group understand and is it addressing the importance of pacing its work and resting? Does the group under-

stand and is it acting on the limits to and impact of growing in complexity and scope?
- Are characteristics of effective teamwork evident in the group's dynamics? Why or why not?

Fragile Relationships

- Is the health and potential fragility of the relationship being carefully and closely monitored?
- If the relationship is becoming fragile, how and by whom are decisions being made about whether it should be saved or dissolved?
- What options are available for saving the relationship and why?
- If a decision is made to dissolve the relationship, are steps being taken to deliberately and carefully plan for its dissolution? Is dissolution being handled professionally so that possibilities for future collaboration are maintained as much as possible?
- Are final arrangements for dissolution being made? By whom?
- Are transition rites being provided so participants can more easily let go of the past and look toward the future?

In addition to drawing our attention to elements of programming that should be evaluated even when collaboration is not involved, these questions identify dimensions of programming that should be added to evaluations of programs planned and offered collaboratively. This brings us to the topic of the interconnected dynamics of program planning and collaboration.

CHAPTER 7

The Interconnected Dynamics of Collaboration and Program Planning

While writing this book, we reviewed the rich and extensive literature of program planning to determine if and how authors made connections between program planning and collaboration. This review resulted in five broad observations about how these two processes are connected in the literature. First, in several cases interorganizational collaboration is not explicitly addressed as a means for planning programs. Rather, this set of literature focuses on the planning of programs within and by a single organization. Second, in other instances collaboration or cosponsorship is mentioned, but little detail is provided about either decisions to collaborate or the processes involved. Goody's and Kozoll's (1995) book presents an example of this approach. Cosponsorship is mentioned as a strategy for the development of programs, and some attention paid to the benefits of collaboration, but very little detail is provided about principles to employ either in deciding to collaborate or in the process itself. Third, collaboration is treated primarily in terms of a strategy to be considered in programming, with particular attention to choosing it as a preferred action strategy. The insights about this choice provided by Cervero (1988, 1992) and Beder (1987), and reviewed in Chapter 1, illustrate this particular focus. Fourth, collaboration is identified as a particular type of program planning, and some dimensions and principles are considered through reference to examples. Houle's (1996) category of collaborative institutional planning, briefly reviewed in Chapter 6, is an example of this approach. So too is Knox's (1993) extensive comparative study of synergistic leadership in program planning in different kinds of programs and in different countries. Both Houle and Knox have provided extensive illustrations of collaboration in program planning. They also identified several dimensions and principles that resonate closely with some of the concepts, strategies, and principles considered here. However, collaboration is not the focal point of their work; rather, it is addressed in terms of its relationship to broader principles and issues of program design and leadership. The program-planning literature is therefore characterized by a great deal of variability in its discussions of the relationship between program planning and collaboration. This variability requires that these two sets of literature be seen as complementary and used in tandem in order to obtain full understanding of collaborative program planning.

This conclusion brings us to our final observation: Collaboration and program planning are parallel but interconnected processes that are informed by both the program planning and collaboration literature. As one example, consider how the different viewpoints on planning described by Cervero and Wilson (1994) relate to themes in this book. Cervero and Wilson identified and described four viewpoints, the classical, the naturalistic, the critical, and their own, negotiation of interests. These viewpoints are particularly instructive because they capture the range of approaches to understanding program planning represented in the program-planning literature.

The first viewpoint Cervero and Wilson described is the classical. The literature that undergirds this viewpoint identifies key questions and issues, such as the purposes of programming, the needs of learners, and the organization of learning experiences that program planners must address. As we reflected on the examples provided by informants, we could see them addressing these issues. But, as Cervero and Wilson have pointed out, these issues were not considered by informants in linear and prescriptive form but as required by contextual factors and practice-based experience and insight.

The naturalistic viewpoint is focused on the judgments of practitioners and the justification for them in specific contexts of practice. This viewpoint is also evident in the examples and information shared by informants. The principles used by informants to make decisions, especially those highlighted in Chapter 5, provide evidence of individual planners deliberating and making difficult decisions about programming and collaboration in specific programming contexts.

The third, or critical, viewpoint addresses political and ethical issues embedded in program planning. It draws our attention to questions about whose interests are served in programming and to the means and ends of programming. Information gained from informants also illustrated the diversity of interests that were present in their work and the ethical issues they confronted.

Finally, Cervero and Wilson, noting the incompleteness of each of these viewpoints, have suggested another. From their perspective, program planning is "a social activity in which people negotiate personal and organizational interests" (p. 4). They not only described the different kinds of interests present in program planning, but also considered issues of power central to the ways different interests can be negotiated. They also provided guidance about different strategies that planners can use to deal with different types of power relationships and interests, with a particular focus on nurturing the democratic planning of programs.

As this book has illustrated, collaborative program planning is truly a social activity, in which meanings are socially constructed and social relations are key to both progress and results. Different interests and relations of power are also present in collaborative programming, as is their negotiation. Although our focus as been primarily on interests, we have also dealt with power, especially the extent to which it is shared among collaborators. However, we have not emphasized power as much as we might have and neither have our examples provided evidence of more democratic forms of planning, in which, for example, potential participants are more substantively involved in planning. Both of these areas seem ripe for further investigation.

Collaboration and program planning therefore relate to each other like the strands of a double helix. The program planning literature describes what needs to be accomplished to plan and develop programs, and provides insights about how that is done. The literature on collaboration, in contrast, concentrates primarily on developing and sustaining relationships among people and organizations through unconventional means of governance, unique forms of leadership, and attention to balance between a variety of tensions.

This book has addressed the strands that link these two processes and thus these two literatures. Collaboration is one of many program-planning strategies. But, as this book has demonstrated, in ways that the program-planning literature does not, it is a strategy that cannot be entered into lightly. Judgments about levels of collaborative intensity required for different programs and situations have added important dimensions to our understanding about choices that must be made when deciding to collaborate. Attention has been drawn to the impact collaboration has on program planning by highlighting the added requirement of relationship building and maintenance to the already complex processes of planning. Although collaboration can contribute much to the effectiveness of planning, as examples have illustrated, it can also constrain planning in significant ways.

Collaboration and program planning are closely related activities but they are not one and the same. Rather, they are parallel processes that affect each other by the ways in which they are connected. This book bridges these processes by identifying principles, practices, and strategies that provide the necessary interface between them.

PRINCIPLES TO GUIDE THINKING ABOUT COLLABORATIVE PROGRAMMING

We have identified six broad principles to guide thinking about collaborative program planning. These are not suggested as prescriptions. Rather, they are meant to identify broad areas that should be recognized and addressed as judgments are made about collaboration.

Collaboration Is Unique for Each Situation

As we have noted, collaborative relationships differ for each unique situation. Judgments about whether to collaborate must be made on the basis of risks, costs, and benefits associated with particular organizations and specific programs. In addition, the intensity of collaboration required and the strategies employed in collaboration will vary according to several factors, including the nature of partner organizations, whether collaboration is mandatory or voluntary, whether it occurs within the context of a formal agreement, and owing to the complexity and scope of the program being planned. Therefore, the principles and strategies discussed thus far should not be viewed as prescriptions. Rather, they should be adapted, just as our informants did, to particular organizational and programming situations as unique collaborative forms are sculpted within specific contexts.

A Historical Perspective Is Essential

Each of our informants has had rich experience in a variety of collaborative programming efforts. It became evident through our discussions with them that they constantly reflected on their experiences to learn about how best to collaborate in current and future programs. They constantly studied themselves and their experiences so they would know, for example, what leadership roles to assume and when, and what strategies were most effective for differing conditions. They were not wedded to a set of behaviors. Rather, they were guided by what experience had taught them about effective courses of action. They learned not only from their successes, but also learned as much or more from difficulties, and even failures. Just as the example of the consulting firm's negative experience in collaborating with the government agency was very valuable in our consideration of several important issues, bad experiences with collaboration can be very instructive. However, history can be a good teacher only if we are vigilant in monitoring and assessing collaborative ventures and reflecting on and learning from our own practice in them.

Collaboration Is Complex and Sophisticated Work

Collaboration entails adapting principles to specific contexts and situations. It requires reflection on action and learning from experience. It calls for sophisticated and difficult judgments in very ambiguous situations. In the best of circumstances, program planning occurs in poorly defined and problematic situations. Collaborating in program planning only adds to the ambiguity and complicates the problematic nature of program planning. Thus, collaboration is as much an art and craft as it is a science. Collaborating is also difficult but rewarding work. The principles outlined in this book are intended to deepen our understanding of collaboration and to provide guidelines that contribute to successful collaborative ventures. But, as the experiences of our informants have indicated, these principles mean little unless there is a deep commitment to this type of program planning, to the hard work that such programming requires, and to the resilience needed to work through the difficulties that will naturally occur.

Collaboration Requires Understanding of Unconventional Forms of Governance

In Chapter 1 we highlighted the fact that a collaborative venture requires the formation of a temporary organization composed of representatives from partner organizations. There and in subsequent chapters we have illustrated how the processes and governance structures of collaboration differ from our conventional views of how our own organizations work. Unique forms of leadership are required, a particular brand of teamwork is necessary, a depth and breadth of communication infrequently used in organizations is needed, and a variety of unique tensions and transformations arise and must be addressed.

Therefore, it is important for collaborators to think differently about collaboration than they think about their own organizations. As we pointed out in Chapter 4, having to think differently and work with individuals outside of our own organization pose a number of risks that we seldom experience in our own organizations. These risks to our ways of thinking, to trust in others, to equity in the relationship, and to the reciprocity we develop with other individuals and organizations call for working in ways that differ from the conventional. Openness to these unconventional ways of working, understanding them and their subtleties as much as possible, and then acting on these understandings, is central to effective collaboration.

Pacing and Rest Are Needed

Collaborating to produce an educational program is much more difficult than working alone. The time required to orchestrate collaboration, the attention to communication, the political strains, and keeping planning on track deplete energy. Collaborating also takes time and energy away from work at one's own organization. There will be times when the work of the collaboration must take precedence, requiring us to request help from colleagues and superiors. Even if the benefit of collaborating is clear to our organizations, questions, irritation, and complaints from colleagues about the effort are possible. Those assigned to a collaborative venture may find themselves working on two jobs for a period of time.

These time demands illustrate the need for adequate pacing and rest both during collaboration and between collaborative efforts. As noted in an earlier chapter, adequate pacing provides team members time not only to reflect on decisions, but also with time to attend to issues and problems in the organizations they represent. A time of rest between collaborative efforts provides additional time for reflection about what was learned from the collaborative activity, but also an opportunity to restore the energy needed for the intensity required in working with other organizations.

Leadership and Vision Are Fundamental

We continued to talk with the informants while we were writing this book, and they constantly emphasized the importance of leadership and vision. As we have noted, the leadership roles performed in collaboration differ in important ways from those we usually associate with leadership in our own organizations. Also, different partners will assume different leadership roles at different stages of collaborative planning. Further, since leadership in collaboration has no basis in authority and little basis in power relations, it is important that leadership be understood as a relationship between leaders and followers.

Leadership in this instance " . . . is a subtle process of mutual influence that fuses thought, feeling, and action to produce collective effort in the service of the purposes of *both* the leader and the led" (Bolman & Deal, 1991, p. 410). Leadership, like the other aspects of collaboration, is therefore both subtle and powerful. It takes into account the constancy of mutual adjustment among partners and the social processes through which meaning, including a program vision is constructed. This form of leadership facilitates the group striking the necessary balance between having a vision and constructing one. It allows leaders to be trusted as they convene a group of collaborators to address a problem domain through programming. It allows various individuals to champion the process with the full support of other partners. And this form of leadership provides the basis upon which members of the group acquiesce to others as strategies are being made.

A compelling and realistic vision is likewise essential. The vision will take different forms for each collaborative situation but it should have several key ingredients. First, it must be both compelling and realistic. Second, its central focus should be on the program and the benefits of participating in it. Third, it should also address, in tone if not in words, the collaborative relationship. If collaboration is indeed a valued programming strategy and if collaboration also possesses inherent benefits for organizations and individuals alike, then capturing these values in a vision contributes not only to the development of the relationship but to future prospects for collaboration. Fourth, it must recognize that developing the vision is no less important than having one in final, written form. As noted several times before, the processes involved in deciding on a vision for programming provide early and continuous avenues for relationship development. In Chapter 1 we highlighted Gray's (1989) observation that the collaborative process is an emergent one. Yet, it is also one that is shaped by people, as relational forms of leadership are performed by partners and as a clear and compelling vision is developed and chosen to guide the effort.

IN CONCLUSION

This book was completed through a collaborative effort. Writing the book in this fashion has made us all the more sensitive to the subtleties of this kind of endeavor and the intensity and hard work required to make it successful. Going alone is certainly the easier, but many benefits are missed. Insights that others might contribute are foregone, friendships are never made, accomplishments are never celebrated in quite the same way, and the benefits of reflecting on and learning about working with others are never fully realized.

We wrote this book together because we are drawn to collaborative efforts and enjoy them. We also wrote the book because we believe collaborative program planning offers many benefits for potential learners, individual collaborators, and the organizations they represent. Deepening our understanding of collaboration and improving practice is therefore important not only for personal and organizational benefit but is even more important for the quality and effectiveness of programs that touch the lives of adults served through these efforts.

APPENDIX

INTERVIEW GUIDE

Please respond to each question, providing examples of specific programs that will enhance and add specificity to your answers. We would be very pleased if you would provide us with written material on programs you have mentioned in your responses.

1. Please begin by providing a brief description of your organization. (This can be similar to the brief descriptions found at the end of Chapter 2. In addition, if this information can be obtained from publicity material that you can provide, it can substitute for your answering this question.)

2. Why does your organization collaborate in the development of educational programs for the audiences or markets you serve? What have been the gains? What are the negative dimensions, if any? What kinds of financial and other costs have been significant when you have collaborated?

3. What do you think are the four to six major reasons that contribute to successful collaborative efforts you have worked on? If you can, relate them to the material on what collaboration requires.

4. When collaboration has been shaky or collapsed, what do you believe were the causes? How do they relate to the enclosed material on challenges to collaboration. What have you done in these situations?

5. Have you identified any danger signs that tell you the collaborative effort is potentially a shaky one? What types of action do you take when those danger signs appear?

6. What different roles have you played in the development of collaborative educational programs? Please be as specific as possible.

7. What have you learned that would be most beneficial to those with little or no experience in collaborating to produce educational programs? Please be specific.

8. How do you believe support for collaboration is maintained? For example, what information do you have to provide to whom in the cosponsoring organizations? How essential are small successes? What would you call a small success? What role does compromise play? Who must be cultivated?

9. How important is a vision of what the group hopes to accomplish? How soon must a vision be established?

10. Could you contrast formal agreements with informal, personal relationships (that include, for example, trust, candid communication and friendship among those working together) established between those who collaborate on a program? When is a formal agreement necessary and when is it a hindrance? How important are trust and strong personal relationships? Please provide examples of when formality was necessary and when informal approaches worked best.

11. What risks must be taken when you collaborate with another organization? How can those risks be minimized?

12. What are the three most important lessons you have learned from working with other organizations?

13. Can you think of an incident in a collaborative experience that was particularly telling and that you remember clearly? Please describe it and what you learned from it that would be of value to the book's readers. (See "Case Study Questions" below for some ideas about what we would appreciate your including in this description. However, do not feel limited by these questions. Other details and information are very welcome and helpful.)

14. What other advice would you suggest to those who must work with other organizations to produce effective educational programs?

CASE STUDY QUESTIONS

In describing your experiences with a particular collaborative programming effort (question 13 above), please be sure to address, at minimum, the following questions.

1. What was the program's topic?
2. Who were the program's major collaborators?
3. Who were the program's anticipated participants?
4. Why did the collaborators choose to work together?
5. What, if any, problems did they encounter as they planned the program? How were those problems resolved?
6. Who performed the major leadership roles and when?
7. Why did the group work well together, or the converse?
8. What was responsible for the program's success, if it succeeded or the converse?
9. What did you learn from this program that you will apply in your future program planning efforts?

REFERENCES

Beder, H. W. (1978). An environmental interaction model for agency development in adult education. *Adult Education*, 28, 176–190.

Beder, H. W. (Ed.). (1984). *Realizing the potential of interorganizational cooperation*. New Directions for Continuing Education, no. 23. San Francisco: Jossey-Bass.

Beder, H. W. (1987). Collaboration as a competitive strategy. In C. Baden (Ed.), *Competitive strategies for continuing education* (pp. 85–95). New Directions for Continuing Education, no. 35. San Francisco: Jossey-Bass.

Benson, J. K. (1975). The interorganizational network as a political economy. *Administrative Science Quarterly, 20,* 229–249.

Bergquist, W., Betwee, J., & Meuel, D. (1995). *Building strategic relationships: How to extend your organization's reach through partnerships, alliances, and joint ventures*. San Francisco: Jossey-Bass.

Bolman, L. G., & Deal, T. E. (1991). *Reframing organizations: Artistry, choice, and leadership*. San Francisco: Jossey-Bass.

Bolman, L. G., & Deal, T. E. (1997). *Reframing organizations: Artistry, choice, and leadership* (2nd ed.). San Francisco: Jossey-Bass.

Boyle, P. G. (1981). *Planning better programs*. New York: McGraw-Hill.

Cervero, R. M. (1988). *Effective continuing education for professionals*. San Francisco: Jossey-Bass.

Cervero, R. M. (1992). Cooperation and collaboration in the field of continuing professional education. In S. Hunt (Ed.), *Professional workers as learners: The scope, problems, and accountability of continuing professional education in the 1990s* (pp. 93–122). Washington, DC: Office of Educational Research and Improvement, U.S. Department of Education.

Cervero, R. M., & Wilson, A. L. (1994). *Planning responsibly for adult education: A guide to negotiating power and interests*. San Francisco: Jossey-Bass.

Colgan, A. H. (1990). Continuing professional education: A study of collaborative relationships in engineering universities and corporations. (Doctoral dissertation, University of Illinois at Urbana-Champaign, 1989). *Dissertation Abstracts International, 50*, 1895A-1896A.

Ferro, T. R. (1990). A revised model of interdependence of providers of continuing professional education. *Proceedings of the 31st Annual Adult Education Research Conference* (pp. 77–82). Athens, GA: University of Georgia Center for Continuing Education.

Fisher, R., & Ury, W. (1981). *Getting to yes.* Boston: Houghton Mifflin.

Goody, A. E., & Kozoll, C. E. (1995). *Program development in continuing education.* Malabar, FL: Krieger.

Gray, B. (1985). Conditions facilitating interorganizational collaboration. *Human Relations, 38* (10), 911–936.

Gray, B. (1989). *Collaborating: Finding common ground for multiparty problems.* San Francisco: Jossey-Bass.

Grotelueschen, A. D. (1980). Program evaluation. In A. B. Knox and Associates, *Developing, administering, and evaluating adult education* (pp. 75–123). San Francisco: Jossey-Bass.

Houle, C. O. (1996). *The design of education* (2nd ed.). San Francisco: Jossey-Bass.

Kanter, R. M. (1994). Collaborative advantage: The art of alliances. *Harvard Business Review,* 72 (4), 96–108.

Katzenbach, J., & Smith, D. (1993). The discipline of teams. *Harvard Business Review, 71* (2), 111–120.

Knox, A. B. (1993). *Strengthening adult and continuing education: A global perspective on synergistic leadership.* San Francisco: Jossey-Bass.

Larson, A. (1992). Network dyads in entrepreneurial settings: A study of the governance of exchange relationships. *Administrative Science Quarterly, 37*, 76–104.

Lawless, M. W., & Moore, R. A. (1989). Interorganizational systems in public service delivery: A new application of the dynamic network framework. *Human Relations,* 42 (12), 1167–1184.

Limerick, D., & Cunnington, B. (1993). *Managing the new organization: A blueprint for networks and strategic alliances.* San Francisco: Jossey-Bass.

Lindsay, C. A., Queeney, D. S., & Smutz, W. D. (1981). *A model and process for university/professional association collaboration.* University Park, PA: The Pennsylvania State University, Division of Planning Studies.

Meyer, J. W., & Rowan, B. (1977). Institutionalized organizations: Formal structure as myth and ceremony. *American Journal of Sociology, 83*, 340-363.

Miles, R., & Snow, C. (1986). Organizations: New concepts for new forms. *California Management Review, 28*(3), 62–73.

Oliver, C. (1990). Determinants of interorganizational relationships: Integration and future directions. *Academy of Management Review, 15* (2), 241-265.

Orton, J. D., & Weick, K. E. (1990). Loosely coupled systems: A reconceptualization. *Academy of Management Review, 15* (2), 203–223.

Ring, P. S., & Van de Ven, A. H. (1994). Developmental processes of cooperative interorganizational relationships. *Academy of Management Review, 19* (1), 90–118.

Schermerhorn, J. R. Jr. (1975). Determinants of interorganizational cooperation. *Academy of Management Review, 18* (4), 846–856.

Scott, W. R. (1987). *Organizations: Rational, natural, and open systems* (2nd ed.). Englewood Cliffs, NJ: Prentice Hall.

Smutz, W. D., & Toombs, W. (1985, April). *Forming university/professional association collaborative relationships: The strategic selection of boundary spanners.* Paper presented at the Annual Meeting of the American Educational Research Association. Chicago, IL.

Tallman, D. E. (1990). An analysis of interdependent relationships in continuing professional education. (Doctoral dissertation, University of Georgia, 1989). *Dissertation Abstracts International, 51*, 384A.

Thorelli, H. B. (1986). Networks: Between markets and hierarchies. *Strategic Management Journal, 7*, 37–51.

INDEX